No More Telling as Teaching

DEAR READERS,

Much like the diet phenomenon *Eat This, Not That*, this series aims to replace some existing practices with approaches that are more effective—healthier, if you will—for our students. We hope to draw attention to practices that have little support in research or professional wisdom and offer alternatives that have greater support. Each text is collaboratively written by authors representing research and practice. Section 1 offers a practitioner's perspective on a practice in need of replacing and helps us understand the challenges, temptations, and misunderstandings that have led us to this ineffective approach. Section 2 provides a researcher's perspective on the lack of research to support the ineffective practice(s) and reviews research supporting better approaches. In Section 3, the author representing a practitioner's perspective gives detailed descriptions of how to implement these better practices. By the end of each book, you will understand both what not to do, and what to do, to improve student learning.

It takes courage to question one's own practice—to shift away from what you may have seen throughout your years in education and toward something new that you may have seen few if any colleagues use. We applaud you for demonstrating that courage and wish you the very best in your journey from this to that.

Best wishes,
—*Ellin Oliver Keene and Nell K. Duke, series editors*

No More
Telling as Teaching

Less Lecture,
More Engaged Learning

CRIS TOVANI

ELIZABETH BIRR MOJE

HEINEMANN
Portsmouth, NH

Heinemann

361 Hanover Street

Portsmouth, NH 03801–3912

www.heinemann.com

Offices and agents throughout the world

The authors and publisher wish to thank those who have generously given permission to reprint borrowed material:

Excerpts from Common Core State Standards © Copyright 2010. National Governors Association Center for Best Practices and Council of Chief State School Officers. All rights reserved.

Figure 3–4: Student Engagement Model adapted from *So What Do They Really Know?* by Cris Tovani. Copyright © 2011 by Cris Tovani. Published by Stenhouse Publishers. Reprinted by permission of the publisher.

Appendix forms from *Do I Really Have to Teach Reading?* by Cris Tovani. Copyright © 2004 by Cris Tovani. Published by Stenhouse Publishers. Reprinted by permission of the publisher.

Library of Congress Cataloging-in-Publication Data

Names: Tovani, Cris, author. | Moje, Elizabeth B., author.
Title: No more telling as teaching : less lecture, more engaged learning /
    Cris Tovani, Elizabeth Birr Moje.
Description: Portsmouth, NH : Heinemann, [2017] | Series: Not this but that |
    Includes bibliographical references.
Identifiers: LCCN 2016055920 | ISBN 9780325092447
Subjects: LCSH: Effective teaching—United States. | High school
    teaching—United States. | Engagement (Philosophy). | Motivation in
    education—United States.
Classification: LCC LB1025.3 .T68 2017 | DDC 373.1102—dc23

LC record available at https://lccn.loc.gov/2016055920

Series editors: Ellin Oliver Keene *and* Nell K. Duke
Editor: Margaret LaRaia
Production editor: Sean Moreau
Cover design: Lisa Fowler
Cover photograph: Getty Images/Fuse
Interior design: Suzanne Heiser
Typesetter: Valerie Levy, Drawing Board Studios
Manufacturing: Veronica Bennett

Printed in the United States of America on acid-free paper
21   20   19   VP   3   4   5

CONTENTS

Introduction Ellin Oliver Keene   vii

SECTION 1 **NOT THIS**

1
A Lecture-Only Approach
Doesn't Ensure Learning
Cris Tovani

Lecturing: A Dirty Word?   3

"But Lecturing Worked for Me"   4

Could We Limit Our Use of Lecture?   6

- *Who Is Doing the Work?*   8

SECTION 2 **WHY NOT? WHAT WORKS?**

12
People Learn Best
Through Multiple Modes
Elizabeth Moje

What Does the Research Say About Lecture-Only Teaching?   18

How People Learn New Information, Ideas, and Perspectives   21

Is There No Place for Lecture in Subject-Matter Learning?   27

- *Research on Lecture in College and University Classrooms*   28

- *Research on Lecture Conducted in Middle and High School Settings*   31

- *Conclusions and Implications of Research on Lectures Versus Other Teaching Approaches*   34

Research on How People Learn Literacy in Secondary Schools   36

- *Working with Students' Knowledge*   36

- *Providing Opportunities for Practice*   37

- *Engaging and Motivating*   38

- *Navigating Many and Varied Contexts*   39

How Contexts Shape What Teachers Can Do   41

- *Structural Features*   42

Conclusions and Implications   43

Section 3 **BUT THAT**

45

**Planning for
Student Engagement**
Cris Tovani

"What Can I Do Instead of Lecture?" 45

- *Behavioral Engagement: How Learners Function* 46

- *Emotional Engagement: Their Hearts Need to Be in It* 47

- *Cognitive Engagement: The Need to Learn* 55

A Model for Generating Student Engagement 57

- *Opening: Sharing Learning Targets So Kids Know Where They're Headed* 60

- *Minilessons/Microlectures: Helping Students Meet the Targets* 66

- *Work Sessions/Conferences: The Heart of the Student Engagement Model* 67

- *Catch and Release: Refocusing and Reteaching* 69

- *Debriefing: Questioning and Reflecting* 70

- *Evaluating the Use of Instructional Time* 70

Problem-Based Learning: Daily Work Matters 75

- *Problem-Based Learning in the English Language Arts* 81

- *Problem-Based Learning Guidelines* 86

The Marriage of Long-Term and Daily Planning 87

Afterword Nell K. Duke 91

Appendix 93

References 97

INTRODUCTION
Ellin Oliver Keene

I have known Cris Tovani for nearly thirty years, as a first-grade teacher, a staff developer for the Public Education & Business Coalition (PEBC) in Denver, a high school teacher, a fellow literacy consultant, and a friend. Years ago, when she told me that she intended to leave PEBC to try our literacy ideas in a high school setting, I shamelessly begged her to stay. Alas, I knew she was right. Few educators are as effective as Cris with both students and adults, and we needed someone to take ideas about engagement into secondary classrooms.

I have had only one opportunity to meet the indefatigable Elizabeth Moje, now Dean of Education at the University of Michigan, but when we decided that Cris and Elizabeth might coauthor this book, I knew it was a perfect match. Indeed, in our first meeting ideas for this book flew around the room. In fact, Cris and Elizabeth exemplified exactly what we want students to do: they immersed themselves in active discourse about a real problem.

The outgrowth of that conversation is this book. I didn't expect to learn so much about engagement in a book about why and how to minimize telling as teaching. Cris and Elizabeth show us that minimizing lecture isn't merely a what-not-to-do for teachers but rather a way to find time and opportunity for students to engage every day in relevant, problem-based work.

Elizabeth shares that "some students are good at behaving like students," and Cris points out that what may look like engagement is actually *compliance*. Kids have fine-tuned the art of looking like they're learning, but too often "care more about the grade than the actual learning, so they play the game." In fact, Elizabeth tells us that "the demand for lecturing is often most prominent among high-achieving students."

Few would argue with the contention that too much lecture is a problem. Most of us experienced it throughout our learning lives and struggle to imagine alternatives that cover all the content we teach. And that leads to Cris' and Elizabeth's extraordinarily practical suggestions.

In Elizabeth's information-packed Section 2, we discover what research supports about true learning, long-term retention, and reapplication of concepts. She helps us find engaging alternatives to lecture that are backed by solid research. This is the long-sought-after guide for instructional coaches and principals to make the case that lecture-only teaching is not effective.

In Section 3, Cris provides practical suggestions for small-group instruction, including a model for reimagining the daily class period. She helps us see how time spent lecturing can turn into powerful, interactive learning experiences in which students inquire into topics they care deeply about. These experiences lead to greater retention of content and more effective transfer of learning. Cris shares how modeling and thinking aloud about tackling a learning challenge work best in ten- to fifteen-minute lessons, leaving students ample time to work together and reflect on their learning. She finally leads us to understand how crucial it is to know students' interests and passions—what she calls the "emotional engagement" component of learning.

Cris leaves us with this thought: "When kids aren't engaged, I ask myself, Do the students know the behavior of learners? Have I given them a way to emotionally connect with me, their peers, and/or the topic? Is the topic compelling? Have I connected it to meaningful work and time-worthy tasks?"

As you answer these questions with colleagues, I hope your discussions will resemble Cris and Elizabeth's first conversation—full of energy, ideas, and hope for reengaging this country's students.

NOT THIS

A Lecture-Only Approach Doesn't Ensure Learning

CRIS TOVANI

Time is every teacher's enemy: there is always more to teach than time to teach it. Every year, educators are asked to add more to our plate; every year, we try to comply. We're not only expected to cover our content and improve students' ability to read and write but also to ensure that students meet the demands of rigorous state and national standards.

Teaching is incredibly complex, and we take our job very seriously. We want to do what is best for our students, and sometimes that means having to make tough decisions. Do we give up content lectures as our primary mode of instruction, knowing that not getting to all the curriculum could put some students at a disadvantage come test time? Or do we lecture on as much subject matter as possible, knowing that some kids are disengaging? At the very least, lecturing to cover content lets us look our administrator in the eye and say, "I taught it." Lecturing can make covering unrealistic amounts of content conceivable, but do we have evidence that students have really learned when this is our main method of instruction?

Recently, I came across a log completed by a preservice teacher who was observing, first, a high school social studies class on modern world history (an elective with a mix of tenth, eleventh, and twelfth graders), and then an English class of all seniors:

Observation 1 (Social Studies Class)

At the beginning of the period, the teacher announced that a movie on Brazil would be presented the following day. He then called on members of the class to read aloud several paragraphs from the course textbook. Then he tried to stimulate a class discussion by asking, "What were the differences between the colonization of Latin America and the colonization of the United States?" When only a few of the kids participated, he finished the class with a lecture. The entire chapter was covered during the class period. The teacher's objective seemed to be to acquaint the class with the customs and background of settlers of Latin America in comparison with settlers of the United States. Attention was not what it could have been. Students didn't confine their talking to the subject.

Observation 2 (English Class)

For the majority of the time, the teacher talked about the novel the students were reading, while they took notes. Afterward, she told me that her goal was to get students writing more, because local universities were reporting that incoming freshman had subpar writing skills. However, because her students didn't seem to be reading at home and some were struggling readers, she felt compelled to go over the assigned pages in class. This took time away from the writing, but she explained that if the students didn't understand the novel, they couldn't write the essay.

These observations were made by my mother on December 20, 1953. I was surprised how little things have changed!

When there is more to teach than time to teach it, taking over is faster than letting students construct meaning on their own. Lecturing at students all the time rather than using it as only one piece of instruction helps teachers plow through content. Year after year, we are asked to participate in various district initiatives (many

For further information on why teachers overuse lecture

see Section 2, page 14.

of which come and go). As class sizes increase and we try to meet the needs of 130 or more students, lecturing is an instructional strategy that remains the same and at least exposes kids to required content.

Lecturing: A Dirty Word?

Let's acknowledge that lecturing in and of itself isn't a bad way to share information, ideas, and points of view, and under the right circumstances some people learn from it. The problem is that when our only instructional method is lecture, we can't tell which students are constructing meaning and which ones are tuning out.

Most of the lectures I listened to as a student were the "fire hose" type. The teacher provides vast amounts of information so rapidly that the students can't possibly take it all in: it's like trying to drink from a fire hose.

But today, I rarely meet teachers who brag that they teach only through lecture. Instead, I hear statements like, "I don't do that stand-and-deliver thing my teachers did. I make my lectures interactive. I call on individual students to share their thinking." This is certainly better than the fire hose lecture, but when this kind of lecture takes up the majority of instructional time, we don't know who is cognitively engaged and who has tuned out.

Sometimes I hear from teachers about how they have carefully crafted their long lectures in the form of stories and lessons to enhance engagement. I do believe that makes for a more engaging lecture, of course, but a lecture couched in narrative works only for students who are emotionally engaged with the topic or the teacher. Those who don't care about the stories or the topic have another chance to disengage.

> Although activities like these can increase the level of engagement and learning, they don't offer students authentic application of the skills and content they're learning. In Section 2, Elizabeth will offer a disciplinary model of learning, and Section 3 will provide some specific examples from my teaching.

Many teachers add "turn and talk" or ask students to take notes during their carefully crafted lectures. Certainly, the layering of those techniques improves the learning potential of a lecture. Some science and math teachers use a "clicker" approach so that more students can see the thinking of their peers in response to a problem or question. This can be effective as long as students are intellectually curious about the topic. But for those who aren't, randomly clicking answers or furiously jotting something down on paper and then talking to a neighbor is an easy way to avoid learning.

I believe that each of these approaches comes from good intentions, and Elizabeth will explain in more detail how these work to some degree in Section 2. As teachers, we want to engage our students in learning but we don't always know the most effective methods for doing so. And, for learners who are ready to hear what we have to share, telling *can* be effective. The problem with lecture-only instruction, however, is that students can too easily fake their learning, and we never know otherwise until we assess. When we rely only on lecture, we are at a disadvantage: while we are talking, it's too hard to tell who is learning, who is stuck, and who has checked out.

"But Lecturing Worked for Me"

Often teachers tell me that lecturing worked for them as students—and if it worked for them, it should work for kids today. I can relate: in some of my classes, being lectured to was effective. In those classes, I had a strong background and/or curiosity, so I was intrigued by what the lecturer had to say. Because my degree required preservice hours in schools, I had the opportunity to try out what I was being told in the lectures.

However, in the classes that I didn't really care about or that I thought were irrelevant but necessary for graduation, lecturing wasn't useful. In those classes, I was engaged behaviorally so as not to draw attention to myself. I put in my seat time and had coping strategies that helped me endure the boredom. Sometimes, I would do work for other classes, then just to show I was "paying attention" ask a timely question designed to make the teacher feel I cared. If the test was short-answer or multiple-choice, I'd make an appointment with the teacher beforehand and ask him what material I should pay attention to. I'd memorize a few facts and drop them into my constructed responses. After a few grades or quizzes, I'd start to pick up on the pattern of grading and adjust my answers for the next assignment.

I learned how to be a teacher pleaser, and every year I got better at gaming the system. Some teachers thought I cared when I didn't. Others thought I was bright and hardworking when I wasn't. The downside to the pedagogy of telling as an instructional mode is that it makes it really hard for the lecturer to tell when and for whom the lecture is effective. The "good" students may be compliant simply to get a good grade and the "bad" students may be off task because they choose not to hide their boredom or confusion. The archaic caste system of secondary schools that places students in tracked courses because of a perceived natural order of intellect or behavior may or may not be accurate. It takes further probing to know if students are learning from the lecture. By covering content through telling, the teacher is controlling how the content is being delivered but isn't controlling how students process, remember, or understand the information.

> If we want students to love math enough to become mathematicians, for example, we need to give them experiences that allow them to inquire as mathematicians. You'll find specific examples of this work in Sections 2 and 3.

For those of us who learned through lecture, several conditions were probably in place. First, the lecturer was an engaging speaker. There are many teachers who are engaging. They've been bitten by the entertainment bug and can often hold kids' attention for short periods of time. Second, we were interested in the topic. Each of us can probably name a handful of students who love our class and may even become teachers themselves, but for the majority that's not the case. Lastly, we had time to apply the information we'd heard. If we don't get time to process, the information is quickly forgotten. When the lecturer is engaging, the topic is relevant, and the learning is immediately applied, some students can benefit from the lecture mode of instruction. Unfortunately, students aren't always enthralled with the subject matter, and if we are lecturing the whole time, there is no room for application. In Section 2, Elizabeth will shed further light on the science of how we learn.

Could We Limit Our Use of Lecture?

Even without the mountains of brain research, we know that people have trouble sitting and listening for extended periods of time. Dr. John Medina, director of the Brain Center for Applied Learning Research at Seattle Pacific University, writes that adults can only listen attentively for ten or so minutes before needing a brain break. Medina (2008) does the math with a typical one-hour lecture: "Before the first quarter-hour is over in a typical presentation, people *usually* have checked out." Medina compares school lectures to a business model and notes, "If keeping someone's interest in a lecture were a business, it would have an 80 percent failure rate" (74). This low success rate makes a compelling case for rethinking how to make better use of class time. Teachers can lecture their socks off but if only a few students are paying attention after ten minutes, what's the point?

It's understandable that to do all that is asked of us we sometimes resort to instructional practices that are more efficient than effective. Unlimited lecturing is efficient but not effective. When I don't intentionally plan the work that students will do in class, I find myself talking at them way more than I intend to. It happens when I underestimate the amount of curriculum I have and I overestimate the time I have to teach it.

Recently, I led a three-day workshop and because I tried to teach more than I had time for, I ended up resorting to talk. Each day I extolled the virtues of letting learners do the work, emphasizing how important it was for teachers to limit their talking so kids could engage and practice critical thinking. Ironically, when it was time to collect the evaluations, one came back that wasn't as glowing as I would have liked. (See Figure 1–1.) This participant would have gotten more out of the institute if I had given her and her colleagues more time to read, write, and discuss their learning. Time got the best of me and I fell into the trap of lecturing. The pressure to cover the "content" drove

Figure 1–1   Evaluation Form

Comrehension Times Three
Denver, July 2012
EVALUATION FORM

	Strongly Agree	Somewhat Agree	No Opinion	Somewhat Disagree	Strongly Disagree
1. The institute increased my knowledge and skills in my areas of certification, endoresement or teaching assignment.		☒	☐	☐	☐
2. The relevance of this activity to teaching standards was clear.	☒	☐	☐	☐	☐
3. It was clear that the activity was presented by persons with education and experience in the subject matter.	☒	☐	☐	☐	☐
4. The material was presented in an organized, easily understood manner.	☐	☒	☐	☐	☐
5. This activity included discussion, critique, or applications of what was presented, observed, learned, or demonstrated	☐	☐	☐	☐	☐

My afternoon breakout sessions were with: _____ Chris T _____
(Stephanie, Debbie, or Chris

The best features of this activity were: Lots of useful strategies and thoughts to inform my teaching. Also seeing that she also has kids that "blow it" on assignments. It's not magically great everyday in her class either.

Suggestions and reactions I wish to offer: Lots of discussion on: teacher → students work but not in practice. felt more teacher talk than us practice, us discuss

Other thoughts and recations I wish to offer: But! I got lots of good things to inform my teaching practices. Thank you. We are not blank slates.

Ouch!

A Lecture-Only Approach Doesn't Ensure Learning **7**

me to talk, so, unfortunately, teachers listened more than they got to apply the information. I can't help but wonder how much of what they heard was forgotten.

Who Is Doing the Work?

Both teachers my mother observed in 1953 made attempts to engage students, but because the teachers were doing the majority of the work, it was difficult to gauge students' thinking. Any form of passive learning—copying notes, watching a video, reading a text to answer previously provided questions, listening to a lecture—doesn't require much participation from the learner. Covering content and ensuring that all students are engaged in learning are two different goals.

We want our students to succeed. When time is short and the focus of instruction is on content rather than critical thinking, it's tempting to take over and tell kids what they should know. Instruction changes when we shift from telling to helping students construct meaning. When we forget what matters most in learning and engage in classroom practices like reading aloud to cover content or lecturing to get through material, we ignore how we learn best. When we do all the work, we unintentionally rob students of their opportunities to learn.

As an instructional coach, one of the first questions I ask is "What matters most to learning?" Here are some common responses:

- I need a chance to mess around with the concept, time to practice.
- I won't work hard if the learning isn't interesting or immediately relevant.
- I need to see the purpose for the learning and how I can apply it.
- I need choice in what I read, write, and practice.
- I want to collaborate with someone who is also invested in the learning.
- I need time to think.

- I need to get and give feedback about my learning so I can redo or revise my thinking or working.
- I want to do real work and figure something out that hasn't already been done.

I've never once had a teacher say they needed a lecture to learn.

When I consider what prompts my own engagement, three things come to mind: I have to know how to behave in a way that is productive to learning; I have to have some emotional connection to the topic or the people I'm learning from and with; and I have to be intellectually stimulated. The engagement of the learners in my classroom is also demonstrated by how they "behave, feel, and think" (Fredricks et al. 2004, 59). The intersection of all three types of engagement (see Figure 1–2) provides many reasons for students to work hard and requires that we plan differently than we do when we lecture.

> Often the challenge for teachers is envisioning a teaching model that reflects these commonsense responses. It's not because they don't have the capacity to do otherwise but rather because the lack of a model has left them trapped into thinking there is only one way to deliver instruction.

Figure 1–2 The Intersection of Three Types of Engagement

Emotional Engagement

Behavioral Engagement

Cognitive Engagement

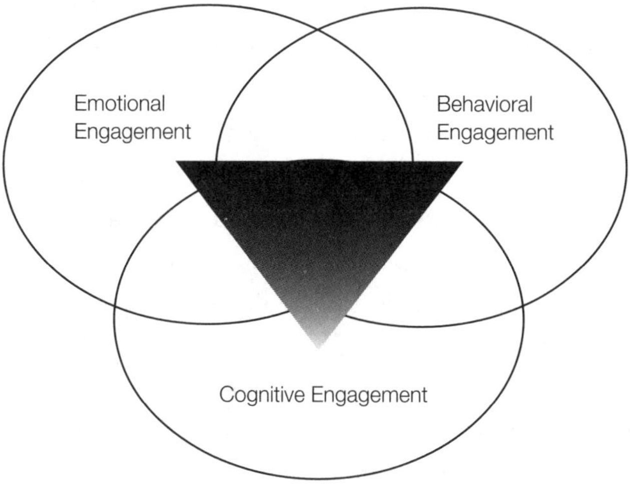

Behavioral engagement targets learners' sense of competence. Students who are behaviorally engaged participate—they respond to the task in obvious ways. They know the behavior that will help them succeed in academic situations. Behaviorally engaged students turn in work on time and apply strategies that enable them to persist when the going gets tough. They ask questions in class and volunteer their thinking.

Emotional engagement targets individuals' need to connect. Learning can begin and be sustained when students have connections to the teacher, their peers, and/or the topic. We cannot underestimate the influence that feelings and emotions have on students when it comes to learning. When we create in our students a sense of belonging to a community or project, students work harder and longer.

Cognitive engagement targets the need to know. When students are cognitively engaged, they see a purpose and a need to uncover information and master concepts. Cognitively engaged learners see how what they are learning is connected to the world outside school. They aren't doing the work for the grade but for the gratification of knowing. Cognitively engaged students are invested in their learning. Fredricks and her colleagues (2004) define this type of engagement by labeling what students do as their "psychological investment in and effort directed toward the learning, understanding, mastering the knowledge, skills or crafts that the academic work is intended to promote" (64).

Giving up or at least minimizing time spent lecturing will be a shock to the system for sure. It means releasing some control and that's scary. But, take heart. There are lots of important aspects of instruction that we are still in charge of. True, we can't control how students think, but we can control how we structure the class period so that kids have opportunities to think. We can't control students' reading levels, but we can provide reading choices so students can access content. Rich text can draw students to the subject area so kids will want to read more about the content. By modeling for students how we, the content experts, think when reading and writing, we inspire students to read and write better and more often on their own. We don't have a lot of say about the adopted state and national standards, but we can plan units that give students meaningful ways to apply the standards before the high-stakes assessments are given.

It's trite to say, but most of us can't work any harder than we already do. We have to work smarter. When we exhaust ourselves lecturing to cover content, we feel we're earning our keep. But in the end, students are suffering as much as we are. Sadly, secondary schools are losing too many kids. According to "Diplomas Count 2012: High School Redesign" (*Education Week*, June 7, 2012), "1.1 million students still fail to earn diplomas." Dropout rates are discouraging and the forecast for producing critical thinkers is gloomy. As a profession, we have to take advantage of the latest, best research we have available to do better by our kids. Our country depends on the job we do with the students sitting before us. We are the ones who will make the difference.

In the next section, University of Michigan researcher Elizabeth Moje synthesizes the research on lecturing and how people learn. She cites studies and examples of why it isn't the most effective way to deliver instruction. Her thinking gives us the impetus to consider other ways to address teaching and learning.

WHY NOT? WHAT WORKS?

People Learn Best Through Multiple Modes

ELIZABETH MOJE

When I started teaching biology and history many years ago, I was eager to engage my students in constructing knowledge about both the natural and social worlds I had studied as an undergraduate. I loved my subjects, and I wanted my students to love learning the ideas as much as I had. I was young and excited to try innovative teaching methods I had learned.

I like to say that I grew up as a teacher during three important moments in education. First, I learned to teach in a time when the available theory and research suggested that people learn best when they are engaged in the work of making knowledge with others, rather than in merely reproducing what others have already discovered or created. I was also deeply invested in progressive perspectives on education, informed by John Dewey and others who argued that *experience* was a key ingredient in learning. And finally, I was a disciple of Paolo Freire, who used the metaphor of banking to critique the typical education practice of lecturing and testing. Freire eloquently theorized that much of education operated like a bank, wherein teachers deposited knowledge in students' minds, and students withdrew that knowledge at the appropriate time to prove that they had learned. School knowledge, in Freire's conceptualization, operated like a form of currency of school, but it had a limited value in the actual world when knowledge had to be put to use. The limitation stemmed from the fact that students had not come to own the knowledge as a result of actively constructing it for themselves. Instead, they were borrowing from the bank and, as borrowers, they accepted ideas as constructed by others.

As a result of the intertwining of these perspectives, I began teaching high school biology and history at the age of twenty-one with a firm commitment to engaging my students in a range of teaching practices such as discussions, simulations, investigations, and writing to learn. I soon learned that my goals were easier to imagine than to enact. What seemed so easy when I read about it in research reports or when experts told me about these ideas in professional development was actually quite difficult to carry out with real fifteen-year-olds hour after hour, day after day, week after week, and year after year. As a result, in my first few years of teaching, I often found myself resorting to telling my students what they needed to know so that we could get on with constructing knowledge. The irony of that was not lost on me, but I struggled with how to do it differently. (As an aside, so, apparently, did John Dewey. Despite Dewey's commitment to experience-based education, Dewey routinely lectured in his university classes. Indeed, he lectured at great length, and, if student reports are to be believed, he did so in a less than engaging manner.)

My struggle to engage my students in something other than telling as teaching and learning as receiving knowledge is what ultimately led me to study literacy teaching and learning. I recognized that I was often resorting to lecture when I found that my students did not under-stand the texts I had hoped they would read. Through my studies I expanded my understanding of cognitive, sociocultural, and criti-cal perspectives on teaching and learning; that expanded knowledge helped me develop teaching practices to put the lecture in its proper place in my classroom. I learned ways to help students build knowledge and relied on small, just-in-time lectures only to help students make sense of ideas they were developing.

What is my point? It is quite simple: My twenty-five years of classroom-based research with teachers and students, together with my thirty-four years of teaching, have yielded extensive data on and experience with why teachers teach as they do. Teachers by and large do not lecture because they like to be in control, or because it makes them feel powerful, or because they want to "plow through content." Those may be artifacts of lecturing or of the pressures teachers often face in middle and high school classrooms, but they are not the reasons teachers lecture. My research documents that most teachers lecture for at least three, often overlapping, reasons.

First, teachers who lecture often do so because they believe that students learn through lecture. They believe lecture to be economical, efficient, and effective. They believe they are doing a service to their students by preparing them with the knowledge they need. Many of them experienced lecture-only formats throughout all their years of schooling and believe that they learned from those formats. (In truth, they may have had many other experiences that bolstered their learning, especially in their major subject areas, but what they recall is the predominant lecture mode of their own school experience.) As one middle school science teacher said to me when I encouraged him to have students brainstorm possible reasons for a particular phenomenon, "Why would I take the time to have them brainstorm when they will just come up with what I could tell them in five minutes and we could move on to more interesting work?" (Moje et al. 2001). Time and time again, I have met teachers who want to get to the "good stuff" and lecture to get there faster.

> These teachers are conscious of time, but perhaps there are other ways of being time-conscious that foster deeper student learning? In Section 3, page 73, Cris will talk about time focused on student learning.

The sense of lecture as efficient and economical is especially heightened for teachers who are held accountable to pacing charts and other approaches to ensuring that teachers are addressing content standards. Thus, rather than seeing this as a problem of teachers desiring to "plow through content," it is important to recognize that teachers are often subject to the pressures of time and accountability that privilege seemingly efficient teaching practices. Anyone who knows how people learn best can recognize that such approaches may be fast but do not result in long-lasting meaningful learning. However, that claim is easier to make than it is to enact when one faces the demand to cover content made by administrators, parents, and even students. I will never forget the eleventh-grade student who expressed her displeasure with my teaching when she faced a standardized test question about a fact from an era we had not yet reached in U.S. history. She felt that I had let her down by not preparing her adequately for the test. As a third-year teacher, I did not know how to respond. I felt torn between my desire to engage my students in meaningful history learning and my desire to meet my students' perceived needs.

A second reason teachers often lecture stems from their perception that their students lack the "necessary knowledge or skills" (Moje and Speyer 2014) needed to engage in an activity such as reading a text. The lack of knowledge or skill is often cited among teachers who teach in settings where their high school students' prior education has been compromised and students are widely thought to be reading four to five grade levels behind their current grade. In one study (Moje and Lewis 2007), a teacher who had immigrated to the United States as a non-English speaker reflected on the fact that she felt compelled to engage in explicit instruction on grammar. She explained that she knew what it was like not to understand or be able to express herself when she first came to the United States; she wanted to make it easier for her students than it was for her. She also felt a sense of urgency for her students to learn because they would face the state tests in the spring. "I have to teach them these skills as quickly as possible or they won't do well on the test and that will hurt them in the long run," she said. This teacher did not necessarily believe that the test was a valid indicator of her students' learning, but she did recognize that the results could have consequences for their futures. Although I was trying to encourage my colleague to engage in a different kind of teaching practice, I was struck by the sense of equity and justice that shaped her decision to lecture. This was not a teacher who lectured because it was easy or because it gave her control. She lectured because she believed it would help her students.

Although a steady diet of lecture may be among the least effective methods to use with students who appear to struggle in school, it becomes easier to understand why teachers may turn to it as a solution when we recognize that many teachers believe it is in the best interests of their students. This is especially likely if they are also teachers who believe that lectures are a reasonable way to learn information efficiently. In other words, when teachers are faced with students they believe have not learned what they need to know—and when students are expected to meet certain standards for subject-matter knowledge and skill—the lecture can seem to be a reasonable way to "catch up students."

Indeed, when Jennifer Speyer and I (Moje and Speyer 2014) realized that our eleventh-grade students did not understand two immigration laws that were central to the point of our problem-based social science unit, it would have been a lot faster for us simply to explain the historical circumstances behind the laws. We chose not to do that because we knew that they would develop a better understanding of the laws by taking them apart and studying the statistics behind the laws, but that meant that we did not achieve our ultimate goals for our two-week unit on immigration. In other words, when students need more scaffolding of knowledge and skill, then trade-offs are required between telling information and constructing understanding. Such trade-offs can represent really difficult choices for teachers who routinely teach students whose skills have been compromised.

Finally, teachers often lecture because their students want them to lecture. It is interesting to note that the demand for lecturing is often most prominent among high-achieving students. In one research study I conducted with colleagues many years ago (Moje, Brozo, and Haas 1994), fourth-year French students resisted our attempts to engage them in a project-based approach to learning French because they had spent years "doing book work" and being told how to speak French. Applying what they knew would, they said, "probably be a better way to learn," but they argued that they didn't have time to do the work required to build French portfolios. The teacher stayed true to her goals despite the students' resistance; as a result, a number of students dropped the class midyear. In other words, students themselves are often members of a learning culture that values lecturing—or a pedagogy of telling (Sizer 1984)—and their responses to teachers' attempts to change that culture matter. It can be difficult, especially for novice teachers, to resist their students' (or other colleagues') desires and expectations for certain kinds of teaching practice. Such an explanation does not make the decision to engage in lecture-only teaching practice a wise one, but it should remind us that teachers do not teach—or make decisions about teaching—in a vacuum. They teach people and they teach people in real social and cultural contexts that shape instructional decision making. This means that the reasons to "buck the trends" have to be really strong and really clear.

In point of fact, there are probably many other reasons that as teachers we are all often seduced into a pedagogy of telling, perhaps even against our better judgment. Even now after so many years of teaching and of studying teaching and learning, I often feel the pull to just tell my students what they need to know. I resist, because I also know—after many years of study—what the research makes clear: People learn best when they can experience many different ways of making meaning and when they grapple with ideas and with texts. But this is hard work, especially in demanding high school settings, where students are many and time is short.

To help colleagues wrestle with the challenges of engaging their students through multiple modes of teaching, I use the rest of the section to present the research on how people learn best, with a special look at any available studies of lecture in relation to other learning modes. I note, however, that in reality, very few people engage in the sole speaker lecture, which makes it difficult to find clean comparative studies. Most people use something that researchers have described an "initiation-response-evaluation" (or I-R-E) or an "initiation-response-feedback" (I-R-F) format. This format involves teachers posing answerable questions, getting responses from students, and then either evaluating or giving feedback. Often, that feedback is extended and becomes a kind of lecture. This is an especially seductive—and deceptive—teaching practice because it can feel like the students are involved and engaged. In truth, it is a pedagogy of telling, where knowledge is held by the teacher and students are meant to absorb or reproduce what the teacher presents.

> **Many teachers would argue that they don't lecture when in fact their instructional model looks like this, a form of lecture. We can push our instruction further than this, and in Section 3, page 58, Cris will share a model of how to do this work.**

Thus, very few studies are dedicated to studying lecture versus some other method, largely because most teachers use a range of methods. As a result, I draw from all the available related research, including experimental studies, studies of college and university settings, and studies of high schools and middle schools. I draw from those studies to put forward some basic principles that teachers can use to guide their decisions about practice. And I offer ideas for how school and district leaders can shape systems to support teachers in engaging in the kind of teaching that research says is most effective: problem-based inquiry instruction.

What Does the Research Say about Lecture-Only Teaching?

Why should we care about whether teachers rely on lecture? People have lectured throughout history, and many teachers claim this is the most efficient way to cover content. And, in fact, in and of itself the lecture is not a bad method for sharing information, ideas, or perspectives. Many people share their thoughts with others through lectures. Because learners can participate in well-framed and well-structured lectures for which they have a clear sense of purpose, it is not the lecture that we challenge but rather a conception of learning that makes the teacher the knowledge disseminator and the students receptacles waiting to be filled. Specifically, we challenge the steady diet of teachers and textbooks (or other media) telling, with students regurgitating what they have been told.

The problem with lecture arises with the idea that the only way for students to learn is for the teacher to engage in what Sizer (1984) referred to as the "pedagogy of telling" or what we refer to as stand-and-deliver pedagogy. In other words, the problem with lecture-only teaching lies in thinking that teaching equals telling and that learning is equivalent to a bank deposit (for more on "banking education," see Freire [1970]) in which teachers tell students information and students deposit the information in the vaults of their brains. Humans do store information, but not in a passive way. People connect new information to existing conceptually organized mental structures, sometimes called *schema* (Anderson and Pearson 1984) or *networks* (Rumelhart et al. 1986). These mental structures become more and more powerful as new connections are built and reinforced through experience.

In addition, learning happens as people use language and other tools to participate in the social and cultural contexts of their everyday lives (Rogoff and Lave 1984; Vygotsky 1986). The child, for example, may use a stick to lift a rock off an object she wants to retrieve and then realize that the stick is a useful tool (i.e., a lever) for heavy lifting. The child may not use the word *lever* or recognize the role of the scientific concepts of *force* and *gravity* in the work done by the lever, but she does know that the stick helps her move the rock, and she is likely to use a stick again in a similar situation. Over time, the child moves from learning the concept through doing (what Vygotsky would refer to as a "spontaneous concept" learned through participation in the world) to more formalized learning experiences (what Vygotsky would refer to as a "scientific concept") learned in academic, or disciplinary, domains.

Formalized learning in the stick-as-lever scenario would include learning the language used by others to name the relevant concept (the relationship between force and gravity that makes a stick work as a simple machine), together with precise descriptions of the conditions necessary for the stick to work as a lever. Such learning also involves coming to understand how people who share similar questions or problems investigate the answers or solutions to those problems and how and why they develop shared ways of talking, reading, and writing about the questions and answers they are working on. This kind of learning is facilitated by participation in problem-solving experiences that help students develop increasingly specialized concepts and language.

You'll find specific examples of this learning in Section 3, page 77.

Moreover, in today's world, students need a wider range of skills than being effective at receiving new information. That skill had greater value when the world was a more static place, but today, in a rapidly changing economy and culture, people need to be able to communicate effectively to collaborate across different backgrounds and experiences if they are to solve the complex problems of today's world. It is not just the speed of communication via technology that demands these skills, but also the pace of discovery and change. To be effective and informed, people need to be able to navigate, assess, and respond to the onslaught of new information, ideas, and perspectives. Content is valuable, but it is not enough. People need also to develop skills and practices for engaging with other people, with ideas, and with new tools and technologies.

The development of these conceptual understandings and meaning-making skills is more serious and more difficult to achieve than a "college- and career-ready" mantra might suggest. Educators have always sought to produce students who are more than receptacles of information, but schools have not always offered the necessary learning opportunities to support that goal; if the goal is for all students to learn to be critical readers, writers, and thinkers and thus productive and generative citizens, then teachers, school leaders, and policy makers need to understand effective practices for helping them learn these skills. And the available evidence shows that a lecture-only—or stand-and-deliver—method is not the most useful for ensuring that students not only take in, but also retain, retrieve, use, and construct new ideas.

In the remainder of this section, I will examine more closely what it means to learn and the available research on how people learn best. I will then examine the research on lecture alone versus other ways of engaging students in learning concepts, skills, processes, and practices in light of what the field knows about how people learn best.

How People Learn New Information, Ideas, and Perspectives

It is probably no surprise to read that the research on how people learn does not support a lecture-only—or a "stand-and-deliver"—approach. The research literature instead suggests that the best way to learn is through a mix of classroom participation structures. Such structures can include projects driven by questions or problems, whole- and small-group discussions, participation in real-world activities that make use of targeted learning skills, the reading and writing of multiple texts, scaffolded interactions with challenging problems, and, yes, even judiciously applied just-in-time lectures (the best are usually interactive).

But there is more to this idea than the participation structures themselves. Any way of organizing instruction can be more or less effective, depending on the view of learning to which teachers—and students—subscribe. A tightly structured "discussion" that is meant to ensure students walk away with three facts is not necessarily a better teaching practice than an interactive "lecture" intended to reach the same goal. In fact, the discussion may actually be a poor choice because it is likely to have taken more time to reach the same goal. The point, then, is not about whether one activity is better than another, but whether teachers understand learning to be a matter of making meaning in purposeful activity by connecting and challenging concepts and skills.

Two reports published by the National Academy of Sciences affirm the finding that *participation in purposefully framed and meaningful learning activities* is important to real learning. *How People Learn*

Elizabeth provides a concise synthesis of these two reports here. The full text of both reports is available free online.

(Bransford 2000) examined research on cognition conducted in a range of settings, including laboratory studies under ideal conditions and parent-child studies in people's homes. *How Students Learn* (Bransford and Donovan 2005) focused more explicitly on the learning that occurs in schools (where conditions are seldom ideal) and included examples of excellent interactive teaching and learning in real classrooms. These volumes represent the best evidence from the collected wisdom of leading scholars of cognition, learning, and the construction of learning environments. Those interested in learning more about the studies that led to the principles outlined below should refer to these longer works, and especially to the second volume, which offers examples of excellent interactive teaching and learning in real classrooms.

How People Learn identifies three key dimensions of well-formed opportunities to learn:

1. Student preconceptions and prior knowledge are engaged, expanded, and refined (14, 15).
2. Students "(a) have a deep foundation of factual knowledge, (b) understand facts and ideas in the context of a conceptual framework, and (c) organize knowledge in ways that facilitate retrieval and application" (16).
3. Students take control of their learning by defining their own learning goals and monitoring their progress toward achieving those goals (a metacognitive approach) (18).

A very well-structured lecture can address points 1 and 2 to some extent, but the third dimension is unlikely to be addressed through lecture alone. Indeed, specific findings in the collected reports support the use of problem-based approaches to ensure deep learning:

- Even young children bring knowledge to new learning situations, and over time they use that knowledge to develop strategies for learning and remembering. When the knowledge students have already constructed from past experience is acknowledged and used as a point of reflection and analysis, students either assimilate or accommodate the new ideas (Piaget 1977).

- Knowledge of and skill with learning strategies develops through *practice* "in the skilled and valued activities of the society in which [students] live" (Bransford 2000, 103). That is, students need to engage in tasks that they can readily see as meaningful or that they can come to understand as relevant and meaningful because they are relevant and meaningful to society.

- Interaction both with peers (Piaget 1977) and with "more knowledgeable others" (Vygotsky 1986) is important to both development and learning. Interactions with peers can challenge one's conceptions if peers disagree or provide other viewpoints or perspectives on a phenomenon. Interactions with more knowledgeable others (both peers and adults) can provide scaffolds and supports necessary for learning. For example, interacting with a teacher or knowledgeable peer can allow teachers and peers to offer a just-in-time explanation or to pose a question that might trigger connections for a student who does not understand a new concept. Such information can serve as a scaffold—a temporary support—for students as they connect new ideas to ideas they have already learned. Research that supports the power of interaction as a tool for learning suggests that lectures can build on and expand prior knowledge but cannot on their own offer the practice and interaction necessary to develop deep and long-lasting knowledge, strategies, and practices for using knowledge.

- Practice needs to be organized and scaffolded (Ericcson, Krampe, and Tesch-Römer 1993); in particular, feedback is necessary for what is learned to be transferred to another learning situation. Most important, the type of feedback a teacher offers matters (Bransford 2000). Feedback should reflect the level or depth of students' understanding so they know where they stand (Chi et al. 1989). In addition, it should help students know "when, where, and how to use the knowledge they are learning" (Bransford 2000). A stand-and-deliver approach alone cannot provide the level of application, practice, and feedback necessary for learning to transfer.

- Too often, motivation is seen as a quality a learner either has or does not have. But the motivation to learn is also related to the value and usefulness of the concepts being studied (Eccles et al. 1983; Wigfield, Eccles, and Rodriguez 1998). Students need to see the usefulness of what they are learning to be able to use the information to impact others. Some students are good at behaving like students—Green (1983) calls this "studenting"—but real learning occurs when they collaborate with peers, discuss and debate, design and solve problems, and complete long-term projects (Blumenfeld et al. 1991; Bransford 2000; Bransford and Donovan 2005; Guthrie and Davis 2003; Guthrie et al. 1996; Guthrie et al. 2006). Lectures that frame problems and prompt students to think about concepts can be highly motivating. In other words, the key features of a motivating teaching practice have less to do with who is talking and for how long, and more to do with whether the ideas being shared are meaningful and inspiring within a larger inquiry frame. Without the opportunity to solve the problems or apply the concepts, however, students are unlikely to engage cognitively or affectively.

- "Research has indicated that transfer across contexts is especially difficult when a subject is taught only in a single context rather than in multiple contexts" (Bjork and Richardson-Klavhen 1989, cited in Bransford 2000, 62). Although problem- and case-based approaches allow students to practice new concepts and skills, they need to transfer what they learn to many and varied contexts (Cobb and Bowers 1999). For example, a problem-based physics and engineering unit on how to design a structure to withstand different weather conditions not only teaches various physical and biological principles but also lets students contextualize and transcend these contexts by designing and testing various structures under various conditions; students both internalize the principles for a given context and generalize these principles in relation to other contexts (Fortus et al. 2004, 2005). Lectures, by contrast, are generally limited to the context in which they occur, which tends to be a context abstracted from the real world of the problem under study, thus making lectures difficult to situate in multiple contexts, except through the telling of multiple examples to convey how the concept is shaped by particular contexts.

The National Research Council (NRC)'s central recommendation for translating what we know about how people learn into school-based teaching practices is to create learning environments that are simultaneously learner-, knowledge-, assessment-, and community-centered (Bransford 2000; Bransford and Donovan 2005). That recommendation translates into employing *inquiry-based* curricula that are meaningful to students. The NRC also encourages forming problem-solving teams in which students work together, learning with and from one another. *How People Learn* (Bransford 2000) posits problem- or inquiry-based approaches that start with learners, build knowledge in meaningful frameworks, continually assess and develop students' learning, and develop learning communities.

Because so many of us did not learn this way, this kind of instruction can be hard to imagine. You'll find specific examples in Section 3 that you can use with your own students.

For example, in my design-based research in Detroit, Jennifer Speyer and I (Moje and Speyer 2008, 2014) designed a unit of instruction on the history of immigration law that asked students to consider the question of whether immigration laws in the United States were equitable to all groups over time. We developed a host of reading, writing, and discussion activities that engaged students with primary source texts (i.e., actual U.S. immigration laws, individuals' journals, media texts, social media, and various data sets of immigration statistics). Throughout the unit we employed whole-group knowledge-building discussions and minilectures, small-group work, individual conversations with students, and a range of literacy teaching strategies to scaffold students' reading and writing of complex texts. Because the central concept of the unit was of immediate significance in the sociopolitical context of the time and because our students worked together to make sense of the laws they were reading, the activities—whether lectures, discussions, or small-group work—were meaningful and purposeful for our learning community. It is critical, however, that the inquiry be framed around real problems or questions of interest in the various disciplines. The tasks should not be merely activities that provide students an opportunity to apply skills; instead, the tasks need to be genuine questions of interest that will allow students to participate in an age-appropriate version of the work that scholars do in various disciplines and fields. Without the legitimate problem/question frame, the tasks are simply school activities. They may be fun or engaging, but they are not necessarily inquiry-based.

How Students Learn (Bransford and Donovan 2005) offers additional examples of these approaches, provided by classroom teachers of language arts, science, social science, and mathematics, in which students collaboratively learn concepts and develop the literacy, process, and metacognitive skills to apply these concepts independently. Although the specifics vary, shared features include (a) forming driving questions anchored in real-world, community-based problems; (b) creating investigations and artifacts; (c) collaborating with students, teachers, and others in the community; and (d) using technological tools (Krajcik et al. 1998).

To this list of features of inquiry-based approaches, I add the practice of *using texts and other literacy and communication tools*. A key aspect of knowledge in the disciplines is the ability to read, write, synthesize, and critique ideas offered in print (Lee and Spratley 2010; Carnegie Corporation of New York's Council on Advancing Adolescent Literacy 2010; Moje 2007; Moje and Speyer 2014; Norris and Phillips 2003a, 2003b; Pearson, Moje, and Greenleaf 2010) —or, in the words of the authors of the Next Generation Science Standards, to "obtain, evaluate, and communicate information" (NGSS Lead States 2013). Some refer to this as content literacy instruction; I think of this as disciplinary literacy (Moje 2007).

> **In the appendix of this book, you'll find a variety of ways of gathering student thinking in response to their reading.**

Subject-area teachers need to provide their students scaffolded opportunities to "do the discipline" and, in the process, learn the literacy practices most commonly associated with the subject area and how these practices apply to other disciplines and to their everyday interactions at home, in the community, and with their peers. History teachers, for example, should raise real questions about the past and then engineer opportunities for students to read, analyze, and debate primary, secondary, and tertiary sources, rather than just read textbooks and listen to lectures that cast history as neat narratives of the past (Moje and Speyer 2008, 2014). These units of instruction should ask students to consider their own communities' history in relation to the history of the communities they study, and develop their own questions tied to those framed by state or local standards, thus motivating legitimate inquiry. Similar problem-based approaches can be developed in other subject areas.

Is There No Place for Lecture in Subject-Matter Learning?

Given the emphasis placed on the value of interactive, problem-based approaches in the two NRC reports, one might reasonably conclude that lecture alone is an ineffective method for ensuring students' learning. The limited research base indicates that such a conclusion would be accurate, to an extent. Might, however, there be room for a lecture in the midst of the kind of "doing the discipline" that I describe here?

What does the research say about the value of lecture and, specifically, lecture-dominant approaches?

In what follows, I examine the available research, limited as it is, in search of definitive findings on the relative value of different approaches. Most of the available studies are of postsecondary settings, which is extremely relevant in an era where secondary school teachers are being exhorted to prepare "college-ready" students. Also worth noting is the fact that a popular trend in universities is a move toward trying to offer more engaged learning opportunities through moves such as "flipping" classrooms or setting up small-group opportunities even within large lecture halls. That said, very little research exists on the efficacy of these approaches, even in the postsecondary settings where these moves are advocated. Moreover, the research that does exist tends to focus on student satisfaction with little attention to what students actually learn in the different modes.

Research on Lecture in College and University Classrooms

Most studies—increasingly conducted at the postsecondary level, where large lecture classes are standard practice—either show no difference or favor interactive and problem-based approaches to learning. Not surprisingly, however, most studies struggle to draw a clear line between a lecture approach and a problem-based approach in large part because so few classrooms operate neatly as one or the other, especially in secondary schools. Postsecondary settings—particularly in the STEM (science, technology, engineering, and mathematics) fields—seem to draw the most interest in comparing lecture approaches to some other form of instruction, probably because of the tendency for professors to use lecture-only approaches in large STEM courses.

Speaking directly to the question of how literacy might play a role in enhancing student learning, Harmon and Pegg (2012) examined the role of literacy strategies in lecture-based instruction in an undergraduate introductory biology class. Lecture topics and information were linked to laboratory investigations through literacy strategies such as mapping content, writing focus questions, charting comparisons, drawing scientific processes, and identifying word-part meanings of biology vocabulary. Scores on a forty-question multiple-choice pre- and posttest improved significantly for students who were taught these literacy strategies, suggesting that if teachers implement content-area literacy strategies in their subject area, students are better able to link what they have learned from a lecture to the problem-based, investigative work undertaken in labs. The study alluded to the idea that if teachers were to implement content-area literacy strategies in their respective subjects, then students will be better able to link what they have learned from lecture-based learning, such as in large lectures, to more problem-based, investigative learning, such as in labs. Thus, the authors promoted a teaching model that employed a combination of both qualities of instruction, rather than either lecture- or problem-based. The authors also identified "the inability to think critically" as one drawback in lecture-based science classes, suggesting that hands-on, problem-based learning helps students gain these necessary critical thinking skills. They argued that students in large lectures "lack solid science background," suggesting that literacy strategies such as writing focus questions and breaking up complicated vocabulary terms into smaller parts help students connect ideas.

Although not a study of lecture compared to problem-based learning per se, a study conducted by Morris (2010) might seem to dampen enthusiasm for nonlecture approaches. Morris evaluated the effectiveness of the traditional lecture-based, in-person classroom compared with a blended classroom module that had online and in-class components. Morris evaluated ninety-four undergraduate business students who were studying the supply chain, a topic that relied on understanding the principles of forecasting and inventory planning, taught earlier in the course.

Morris administered a pre- and posttest on the students' knowledge and problem-solving skills relative to forecasting and inventory planning. Differences in learning outcomes between the traditional and blended instruction were not statistically significant. Morris speculated that the only reason the blended model produced better learning outcomes in previous studies was that students had been able to review the material closer to the exam. However, it is also possible that the alternative approaches were simply telling in a different form: watching a video, reading a textbook, and other passive or receptive modes of delivering information are akin to lecturing, and an engaging interactive lecture can develop knowledge and skill better than passive nonlecture instruction.

One of the most compelling postsecondary studies of the value of a lecture is a meta-analysis[1] of 225 previously conducted studies published in the *Proceedings of the National Academy of Sciences.* Freeman et al. (2014) compared the examination scores and failure rates of STEM[2] university students who learned in traditional lecture settings with those who took classes that included "active learning interventions": solving problems in groups, completing worksheets or tutorials during class, using personal response systems (with or without peer instruction), and engaging in studio or workshop activities. They found that average examination scores improved by 6 percent in the active learning sections; students in lecture settings were 1.5 times more likely to fail than students in active learning classrooms. The students in active learning sections outperformed those in lecture sections on all types of examinations, but scored even higher on "concept inventories," which the researchers describe as being designed to "diagnose known misconceptions." In other words, the active learning students performed better on both content and process skills valued in STEM disciplines. This meta-analysis reflects a current trend in university settings to find ways

---

1. Meta-analysts limit the studies they include to fit the parameters of carefully conducted research. Researchers then apply a statistical procedure to assess whether the results of the individual studies add up to powerful findings when viewed as a whole.

2. In this study, STEM included the following disciplines: biology, chemistry, computer science, engineering, geology, mathematics, physics, and psychology.

to move out of the 400-person lecture hall and offer more action-based, immersive learning environments for students (Berrett 2012). This point is one that secondary school teachers and school leaders should consider carefully as they heed the call to prepare "college-ready" graduates. Now more than ever, college-ready students may need to be able to learn by solving problems in collaborative teams.

Research on Lecture Conducted in Middle and High School Settings

There is much less research regarding learning from lectures in secondary schools, partly because so few teachers take a lecture-only approach and partly because it is much more difficult to conduct large-scale, randomized, controlled research there. However, the studies suggest a general trend. Ward and Lee (2004) evaluated the effectiveness of problem-based learning compared with traditional, lecture-based instruction, focusing on seventy-nine high school students in grades 9 through 12 who were taking one of four food and nutrition classes taught by the same teacher. The teacher employed problem-based learning in two of the four classes (forty-two students), and lecture-based instruction in the remaining two classes (thirty-seven students). Using the standardized North Carolina state test on food and nutrition as a pretest and posttest in all four classes, the authors found no significant difference in test scores. However, students in the problem-based learning group demonstrated, by the questions they asked and the critical thinking skills they exhibited, a greater understanding of the connection between the "content, the work world, and their personal lives" (75). Because they were more or less investigators of the topics covered, students in the problem-based learning group may have felt a greater sense of identity with and inclusion in the nutrition community.

Day and Wong (2009) studied two Hong Kong secondary science classes of approximately forty students each. The classes covered the same topics, human reproduction and density. The researchers administered three tests: a pretest to determine students' prior knowledge of human reproduction and density, a posttest to test their knowledge of the two topics, and a delayed posttest to determine their retention of the material over time. The test questions (multiple choice and short answer) were the same for each test. There was no significant difference in the students' test scores between the pretest and immediate posttest on human reproduction, but students in the problem-based learning group outperformed students in the tests on density.

Day and Wong (2009) noted that the students were less motivated to learn about density than reproduction; that the problem-based learning group scored better on this topic suggests that framing and investigating the problem made this topic more interesting and engaging, yielding better results. The problem-based learning group also demonstrated a greater improvement in "comprehension and application of knowledge" over an extended period.

What makes these results especially compelling is the Hong Kong learning context: Hong Kong has a long history of traditional, lecture-based teaching in the classroom, and their schools rarely use problem-based learning. The students in this study were accustomed to Hong Kong's teaching standards; those in the problem-based learning group had never been exposed to problem-based learning and had always been in a classroom in which the teacher instructed rather than facilitated. Thus, the study clearly supports the hypothesis that problem-based instruction is as effective as lecture-based instruction in helping students meet test objectives and suggests that problem-based learning may help students retain information over longer periods.

Finally, a long-term curriculum intervention project undertaken in several U.S. cities suggests that middle-school students who received problem-based science instruction benefited over peers who did not. One urban district compared the state standardized science test scores of 1,803 seventh and eighth graders who participated in the problem-based learning science curriculum with a comparison group of 17,562 seventh and eighth graders in the same school district. Results showed significantly higher achievement for the problem-based learning students and a closing of the achievement gap by male students[3] (Geier et al. 2008). It should be noted that the "control" sample of more than 17,000 students did not necessarily experience a steady diet of lecture-only teaching; some may even have been in problem-based or inquiry-based science classrooms. However, the problem-based learning curriculum units were tied to "driving questions" that linked the instruction to state content benchmarks *and* to documented student interests. The units also employed deliberate and carefully sequenced opportunities for firsthand investigation coupled with secondhand investigations (Palincsar and Magnusson 2001) that featured reading, writing, and classroom discussions.

Although the preponderance of research supports interactive and problem-based approaches, one study (Schwerdt and Wuppermann 2011) claimed the lecture approach was superior in secondary schools based on data from the Trends in International Mathematics and Science Study (TIMSS). Schwerdt and Wupperman isolated the various teaching practices of the teachers studied in TIMSS and then compared standardized test scores. Students whose teachers predominantly used lecture had higher test scores than students of teachers who reported using used problem-based approaches. The study, however, had several weaknesses. The analysis was carried out after the fact (i.e., the data were not collected to compare lecture approaches with other ways of teaching); the analysis included a small number of observations and did little to discriminate how teachers carried out instruction (most of the data came from teachers' self-reporting); and it failed to account for cultural differences that might make various approaches more or less difficult to implement (for example, problem-based approaches introduced in settings where students are expected

---

3. In aggregated data relative to middle school students' science and mathematics achievement, girls often begin to show diminished achievement when compared with boys of the same age. Disaggregating achievement data by race and region, however, shows that in many urban settings with homogeneous African American populations, boys tend to lag behind girls (Lynch 2000).

to sit silently and wait to be given information cannot be adequately compared with a lecture approach or any other).

Most important is the critique that the study measured learning solely in terms of standardized test outcomes. Some argue that such tests are not evidence of learning but performances in a moment in time. If test scores are the gold standard for measuring learning, lecture-based approaches will, in the short term, produce the most uniform—and perhaps the best—result, because the teacher controls the information and the pace with which information is handed to students. Interactive, problem-based approaches, by contrast, engage the learner in constructing knowledge and understanding. A test measuring the knowledge considered valuable by the test maker may not tap all the understanding students possess. It can therefore be argued that lecture-based approaches are the best tool for ensuring high achievement as measured by tests, but not, perhaps, the kind of learning that will last a lifetime.

Nevertheless, the majority of studies I reviewed demonstrate strong positive results on both standard and nonstandard measures for students who were taught with interactive, problem-based approaches. This suggests that problem-based approaches may be even more effective when evaluated on the basis of assessments that account for the kind of learning one expects to occur from inquiry: how to think and reason critically, how to read for varied interpretations, and how to write evidence-based arguments.

Conclusions and Implications of Research on Lecture Versus Other Teaching Approaches

Interactive, problem-based methods that offer students a reason to learn and help them construct knowledge from investigations, materials, texts, and one another are at least equal to the learning that occurs in lecture-dominated classrooms and in many cases offer a statistically significant advantage over lectures. It is true, however, that most of the research on the efficacy of lecture methods when compared to other methods is quasi-experimental or correlational; that is, I was unable to find any studies that assigned students randomly to different teaching conditions and controlled the practices used, which is considered the gold standard for determining whether one practice is superior to another. Also, most of the available comparative studies were conducted at the university level, with an emphasis on large natural science and mathematics classrooms (which are often lecture-style courses). There are a few K–12 studies, but they rarely position their comparisons in relation to lecture-only formats (most studies compare an intervention to teaching that could be considered "business as usual"). Nevertheless, when one considers the evidence about how people learn, together with the evidence, albeit limited, about classroom-based interactive approaches, then it seems clear that lecture-only approaches will not help middle and high school students learn most effectively. Moreover, if colleges and universities are attempting to move toward more problem-based approaches as a result of their research, then K–12 educators need to prepare their students for those approaches.

In sum, lectures are a useful way to teach as long as they are used as one tool in a larger kit of instructional practices. When a rich and compelling frame is provided for learning and students' prior knowledge is tapped, lectures can offer information "just in time" and help students learn necessary skills. In a study conducted in middle-school English language arts classrooms (Moje, Willes, and Fassio 2001), my colleagues and I found that well-placed minilessons on

> **The argument of this book is not that lecture is bad, but that lecture as the only method of instruction is far less effective than other methods of teaching.**

skills such as using dialogue to enhance narrative writing (and using the quotation marks that signify speech) had a dramatic impact on students' writing: they practiced the idea immediately in their own writing. However, when lectures turn into daily stand-and-deliver practice, the effects are not as positive.

Research on How People Learn Literacy in Secondary Schools

Four practices are especially useful in improving students' abilities to comprehend and compose texts in the content areas: (1) connecting to and developing knowledge students bring to the classroom, (2) providing opportunities for scaffolded practice, (3) motivating and engaging learners, and (4) supporting students in navigating the subject areas and their lives outside school.

Working with Students' Knowledge

Patricia Alexander and her colleagues have conducted extensive research on learning from texts in specialized domains (Alexander 1998; Alexander and Jetton 2000; Alexander and Judy 1988; Alexander, Kulikowich, and Schulze 1994). For Alexander, a critical dimension in making meaning from texts is *bridging knowledge*, which I refer to as *necessary knowledge* (Moje 2010).

It is one thing to recognize that students bring knowledge to learning (Bransford 2000); it is another to use that knowledge in teaching (Bransford and Donovan 2005); and it is still another to help students recognize the knowledge they need to understand a given text, whether it be print on paper, a digital image, or an oral lecture or discussion. Some strategies for developing necessary knowledge are discussed below, as well as in the next section.

Project CRISS—Creating Independence Through Student-Owned Strategies—provides professional development showing secondary and late elementary teachers how to help their students integrate new knowledge with existing knowledge as they discuss, write about, organize, and analyze a text's structure and meaning. Students construct knowledge using various reading comprehension strategies: drawing on background knowledge, questioning while reading, organizing the main concepts in the text graphically, and summarizing the text's big ideas. Two studies of Project CRISS' positive effects on reading comprehension in grades 4–6

(Horsfall and Santa 1994; James-Burdumy et al. 2009) meet What Works Clearinghouse standards for potentially positive effects on comprehension, but it is unclear whether the studies were related to comprehension of content area texts or reading comprehension in general. Project CRISS has not been studied at the high school level.

An approach called Reading Apprenticeship (Schoenbach et al. 1999) offers subject-area embedded literacy teaching practices explicitly focused on developing students' metacognitive awareness by "talking to the text" as they grapple with subject-area texts. This talking-to-the-text strategy is similar to questioning the author: students converse with themselves and with others about the sense they are making of text. The focus is on making thinking while reading visible to everyone in the class, thus improving metacognition, which in turn improves outcomes. According to the What Works Clearinghouse, one study of *RA* (Kemple et al. 2008) fell within their standards, providing compelling evidence that RA has a positive impact on student literacy and content learning when enacted with fidelity. The study included over 2,000 ninth graders in seventeen high schools located in ten school districts in various parts of the United States. Greenleaf, Schoenbach, and colleagues have conducted other studies that also show support for the RA practices (Greenleaf et al. 2001; Greenleaf et al. 2009).

Providing Opportunities for Practice

Many discussions of literacy strategies imply that practice is necessary if the strategies are to become regular routines in skilled subject-matter reading and writing, but only a few state this explicitly. One is reciprocal teaching, which also has strong research support. In this strategy the teacher and students take turns leading a dialogue about a text. The teacher begins by

In Section 3, Cris will provide a daily instructional model that devotes the largest portion of time to student practice.

modeling how to ask questions, summarize thinking, clarify under-standing, and predict what he or she might read or learn next in the text—all basic comprehension skills that are automatic in a strong reader. The teacher encourages students to practice by regularly having them take on the role of moderator and modeler, which may be the main reason the strategy is so successful. Annemarie Palincsar, who created the strategy, documented its effectiveness years ago (Palincsar and Brown 1984), but numerous studies since have found it has a positive impact on student literacy in content areas. What Works Clearinghouse gives reciprocal teaching a high effectiveness rating, even after eliminating the vast majority of the more than 165 studies reviewed because they did not fit the WWC's protocol. However, the majority of the studies have been conducted with students in grades 4–8; less is known about how the strategy fares with high school students—especially those who already read well in some subjects but who may need scaffolding for reading advanced texts.

Engaging and Motivating

Many literacy teaching strategies are described as engaging, large-ly because they set purposes for reading or writing about a text. Concept-Oriented Reading Instruction (CORI) (Guthrie, Wigfield, and Perencevich 2004) was expressly developed to spark motivation and sustained engagement. CORI focuses on reading strategies—questioning, activating background knowledge, searching for information, summarizing, and synthesizing information to communicate it to others. CORI has been tested mostly with elementary school students, although some recent research has been conducted with seventh-graders in reading/language arts classrooms. In CORI, elementary school students conduct firsthand inquiries related to a specific topic while also learning reading skills and strategies, peer collaboration skills, and how to produce public communication. Evidence from multiple quasi-experimental studies suggests that CORI instruction/curriculum increases young students' strategy use, conceptual learning, motivation, and text comprehension compared to control classrooms with separate science and literacy curricula and/or strategy-oriented reading curricula (Guthrie et al. 1996). However, although recent studies of seventh-grade students (Guthrie, Mason-Singh, and Coddington 2012) showed improved interest in reading information books, together with greater dedication to keep reading to find information, results also showed decreases in literacy comprehension and in making inferences. Moreover, the fact that CORI was tested in reading/language arts classrooms raises questions about its applicability to middle and high school subject matter areas. Most important, Guthrie, Mason-Singh, and Coddington (2012) themselves suggest that the improved motivation results cannot be extrapolated to high school students because it is difficult to know what other motivational factors might be at work in those contexts (189).

Navigating Many and Varied Contexts

As explained in the research from *How People Learn* (Bransford 2000), the best teaching supports learners to transfer what they have learned from one context to another. Unfortunately, very little research is available on how teachers help students learn to transfer, or navigate, across multiple contexts, especially in secondary schools, which are notorious for constructing departmental silos. Teachers rarely have time to speak, let alone collaborate and plan instruction. We therefore need to extrapolate from other studies. In particular, *How People Learn* (Bransford 2000) and *How Students Learn* (Bransford and Donovan 2005) discuss the results of several studies in science and mathematics in which teachers and researchers created project-based learning curricula that engaged students in transferring their learning to other contexts (Bransford et al. 1998; Cognition and Technology Group at Vanderbilt 1997). In a similar study of project-based science units that my colleagues and I conducted in several Detroit middle schools, students struggled with context-specific references to their environment.

The curriculum designers consequently expanded the examples and project research opportunities to include a range of locales, with a focus on identifying similarities and differences. This helped the students navigate both familiar and unfamiliar terrain (Moje et al. 2001). We asked students when, why, and how various representations (an equation versus a table versus a sentence, for example) and discourse practices (a scientific explanation versus an explanation to one's mother) should be used or avoided. Students were highly engaged in these conversations and made situation-appropriate shifts in their written work, such as writing an explanation of a scientific phenomenon differently when directed to write for other scientists and when directed to write for their mothers (Moje et al. 2004).

Despite research evidence to support the use of these teaching practices, the majority of practices and programs I have described were conducted with young adolescents and do not foreground disciplinary knowledge in ways that invite subject-matter teachers into interactive literacy-rich subject matter teaching (Moje 2008). All of the approaches address both student knowledge and necessary knowledge to be developed, but few explicitly call upon the unique practices of a given discipline to consider, for example, how the knowledge historians need to make sense of various text forms (Wineburg 1998) might differ from the knowledge needed by mathematicians to address a problem mathematically (Bass 2006). What's more, none of these strategies is embedded in problem-based curricula as suggested by the National Research Council reports reviewed previously.

Many of these curricular interventions have yet to be tested for efficacy, but design experiments and small-scale interventions in the disciplines show promise in bringing together the knowledge and practices valued in the disciplines with the strategic practices related to students' reading, writing, and communicating in these disciplines (Bain 2005; De La Paz 2005; Geier et al. 2008; Moje and Speyer 2014; Monte-Sano, De La Paz, and Felton 2014; Smagorinsky 2014). In each case, the teaching routines and practices represent some version of the following: (1) engaging students in the practices of the discipline (e.g., framing a problem, investigating, analyzing data); (2) eliciting and acquiring the necessary knowledge to carry out those practices using content literacy strategies as tools; (3) examining the words, phrases, and discourses that enable disciplinary work; and (4) evaluating why, when, and how disciplinary language and discourses are useful and why, when, and how they are not (Moje 2015). These routines and practices structure and guide daily classroom practice.

How Contexts Shape What Teachers Can Do

With all the theory and research reviewed to this point in the chapter that show the effectiveness of interactive, especially problem-based, pedagogy, why do so few teachers engage in such practice? Research sheds some light on that. First, teachers often do use a combination or variety of instructional strategies—not just lecture—but all of them have a telling or vessel-filling emphasis. Specifically, teachers usually combine three participation structures: (1) lectures, on which students are expected to take notes, (2) recitations (where a teacher asks a question, receives a student response, and then evaluates the response as right or wrong), and (3) student seat work, either high-order knowledge construction tasks or literal-level question-and-answer tasks (Alozie, Moje, and Krajcik 2010; Anyon 1981; Dillon 1989; Dillon, O'Brien, and Volkman 2001; Goodlad 1984; Moje et al. 2011; Sizer 2004; Wade and Moje 2000).

Teachers choose these formats for many reasons: their own learning histories and teaching models (Holt-Reynolds 1992); their beliefs about learning (epistemologies) and teaching (pedagogies) (Douglas, Bain, and Moje 2009; O'Brien and Stewart 1990; O'Brien, Stewart, and Moje 1995); the time and resources available (Moje and Speyer 2014); what they believe they can accomplish given the available time, resources, and accountability requirements (Holt-Reynolds 1992; Sizer 2004); and what they know about designing and managing instructional tasks (Moje 1996; O'Brien, Stewart, and Moje 1995; Sturtevant, Duling, and Parson 2000). Perhaps they don't admit to it in interviews or on surveys, but I have found no evidence that teachers lecture, listen to student recitations, or assign exercises because they think doing so is easy or because they do not care about student learning and engagement.

Although teachers' knowledge (Bransford 2000) and beliefs or values (O'Brien, Stewart, and Moje 1995) partially explain their reliance on a pedagogy of telling despite overwhelming evidence that it is ineffective, another challenge is that secondary school contexts generally do not support, and sometimes even prohibit, problem-based practices. Several types of contextual features of secondary schooling, including both cultural and structural features, challenge the enactment of engaged, action-based teaching and learning and actually promote lecturing. Indeed, much of the solution rests with policy makers and district and school leaders, not with classroom teachers.

Structural Features

One structural deterrent is timing. Classes are generally brief (fifty or sixty minutes), and many separate and distinct classes are crammed into the day. Students and teachers run from one class to another, with no time to process ideas. Moreover, young people are denied opportunities to do the thing they crave most: talk with their friends. Most adults enjoy, even thrive, on casual conversations with their coworkers and would probably be enormously frustrated if they were routinely denied those opportunities, but schools deny that possibility to both students and teachers. Class becomes a constant battle over content learning versus social networking.

In addition, numerous interruptions occur in secondary school settings, from late arrivals to public address announcements to all-school meetings. According to Anyon (1981), working-class and high-poverty schools experience even more interruptions than middle-class, upper-middle-class, and elite schools, which makes interactive, problem-based approaches even more challenging. Student attendance is also often a problem, particularly in economically stressed communities, where transportation to and from school is unreliable, minimal, or non-existent (Moje and Speyer 2008). Worse, late arrivers are often required to wait in detention rooms until a new class period begins. Without consistent attendance, problem-based instruction is extremely difficult because each day's learning is the basis for the next.

Considering accountability demands, district-monitored pacing calendars, and bloated and repetitive content standards, it's little wonder so many teachers resort to a pedagogy of telling, especially because this approach is probably the one they experienced in their own secondary and postsecondary schooling. Changing these practices will take more than teachers' acceptance of learning theories and research evidence; school structures need to change so that the culture of teaching and learning can change. At least some of these changes are the responsibility of administrators and curriculum developers. Without this structural support, a pedagogy of participation will find its way into very few schools.

Conclusions and Implications

People learn best when their existing ideas are engaged, when they encounter an abundance of information and ideas in a situated framework, and when they can reflect on what and how they are learning. They need to actively construct knowledge and build a sense of agency and purpose for their learning. Lectures can be efficient and effective ways of offering people information, especially if the lecturer is engaging and the topic is highly circumscribed or provides technical, concrete, just-in-time information that allows learners to spend their time and energy constructing knowledge around challenging or abstract concepts. Most secondary school teachers do not use the lecture as their sole means of teaching. And yet, too many practice the pedagogy of telling, accomplished through some lecturing, some recitation (in which they pose known-answer questions and students respond to demonstrate their knowledge), and some written work (often drawn from textbooks that present knowledge as given and immutable). This pedagogy of telling not only fails to engage many students but also fails to teach fully integrated concepts and sophisticated skills with which to advance their future learning independently. Many students leave secondary school not ready for postsecondary learning, for vocations and careers, or for lives as productive citizens because they are not engaged in the deepest and most robust forms of learning.

Researchers and practitioners have developed and tested teaching tools, strategies, and practices that scaffold student literacy and content learning. The next section discusses some of them and how they play out in real classrooms.

BUT THAT

Planning for Student Engagement

CRIS TOVANI

"What Can I Do Instead of Lecture?"

In Sections 1 and 2, Elizabeth and I support our claim that even the cleverest lecture can't guarantee learning. As Elizabeth explains, "the available evidence shows that a lecture-only—or stand-and-deliver—method is not the most useful for ensuring that students not only take in, but also retain, retrieve, use, and construct new ideas." She shares powerful evidence that teachers can increase student learning by planning meaningful activities for students' purposeful participation. *Purposeful* and *meaningful* define how activities and participation function for students—how they engage in learning. But it's hard to change our practice without a model, and there is more than one way this work can be done.

What you now have are research principles to evaluate any program or teaching model for efficacy. In this section I'll show you one model that realizes the principles of Elizabeth's research synthesis. It's meant to inspire but not limit your own teaching so that student engagement becomes the centerpiece to your instruction.

The biggest shift you may find if you're using lecture-only instruction is planning for more time for students to participate to increase learning. When students work for sustained periods of time, they get to experience a lot of rich learning. When planning, the intent is to shift how time is used daily to engage more students in active learning opportunities for longer periods of time. In the previous section, Elizabeth defines this as organized, scaffolded practice with feedback that can be transferred to other learning situations. This focus creates momentum for students' engagement to increase over time.

Engagement sometimes gets confused with entertainment. We don't want students just to be entertained, we want them to learn. When I think about engaged learning, I consider what students need behaviorally, emotionally, and cognitively. When all three types of engagement intersect, students have a greater psychological drive to learn for learning's sake.

Behavioral Engagement: How Learners Function

When I work with principals, I tell them that their observations shouldn't focus too heavily on behavioral engagement. Here's why. Behavioral engagement can often be disguised as compliance. Compliance isn't the same as engagement.

Students who are only behaviorally engaged demonstrate that they know the rules of academic learning and want to avoid the negative consequences of not adhering to those rules. They tend to care more about the grade than the actual learning, so they play the game. They seek out the teacher to get more points when their grade teeters between an A and a B. Students know it irritates the teacher to get up and stroll around the room while she is giving directions, so they don't do it. They are careful to format papers correctly.

Instead of reading the novel, students may use tools like SparkNotes to save time and ensure they get the "right" answer. They've figured out what we want and what they have to do to get the grade they need. This doesn't mean they always flourish as learners. Teaching through lecture alone often means that we're planning solely for behavioral engagement and this single focus risks disengaging the students who don't know or care about behaving the way we want.

Of course, we don't give up establishing rituals and routines that make the classroom run smoothly (see Figure 3–1). We still identify behavior that will help students be academically successful and model strategies to help them reengage. We help them know how to be life-long learners. However, we are kidding ourselves if we think that clear expectations and posted rules will engage all students all the time. It won't. We have to plan for emotional and cognitive engagement as well.

Emotional Engagement: Their Hearts Need to Be in It

Most teachers learn early in their career that building relationships with students is crucial. A positive teacher-student relationship enables students to take more risks in their learning and try harder when the work gets tough. Engaging learners at the emotional level has always been my strong suit. I can usually connect with the kids who don't have a strong connection to the school or their peers. When I think about how I engage these types of learners, four core beliefs come to mind that drive my practice (Figure 3–2).

Figure 3–1 Teaching Practices That Support Behavioral Engagement

- Golden Rule: Show students how to get unstuck so they don't quit.

- Identify what you can't live with as a teacher and set up a way for kids to solve the problem without you. (I hate being asked for a pencil. I collect and save pencils in a box kept in the corner of the room. When these pencils are gone, students ask a classmate for one.)

- Model how to work with peers. How do students form groups? What do they do when they don't like someone in their discussion group? How do they talk in small groups? How do they ask for help?

- Establish clear procedures for storing student work folders, turning in work, returning work. Set up an area where reading and writing materials are kept.

- Establish how students will catch up on work they've missed. Decide how you will reintegrate students who get to class late. Explain what students need to do to get busy learning.

- Display both daily and long-term learning targets where kids can see them. Refer to these targets often.

- Think aloud to model how to read (an excerpt from a novel, a primary document, whatever students are dealing with), write, and solve problems.

- Be predictable, so kids know what to expect. For example, my classes start with students silently reading the day's learning targets and matched assessments. Students also know that in every class period they will get time to read, write, and discuss. When I avoid springing surprises on students, they take more risks with new learning.

Figure 3–2 Four Core Beliefs About Students

1. *Students would if they could.* No kid gets up in the morning, looks in the mirror, and says, "Wow, I hope I do terrible today." Teenagers want to be successful. When they quit, it's usually because they don't know what else to do. They act out or avoid work to disguise their confusion. Most teens, especially young men, would rather look lazy or be labeled the class clown than look dumb. A simple—and amazingly effective—question to ask students who are stuck, angry, or disengaged is, "What do you need?" More often than not, they'll tell you. Sometimes they just need some sticky notes to hold their thinking. Other times, they need a clearer explanation of what to do. Perhaps they feel like an outsider. Maybe they need to know why the work matters. Asking students what they need shows empathy and concern for their learning. It's not a passive-aggressive nudge back on track. I'm truly curious about how I can help them reengage with their learning. I want to help them figure out how to get unstuck.

2. *I need to model more.* Students who respond to "What do you need?" with "I don't know" may not be familiar with the available options. Nine times out of ten, when kids fail it's because I haven't modeled enough. Sometimes I think I've been very clear about what I want students to do when, in truth, I haven't. Other times, I've forgotten what it was like when I learned the skill or read the book the first time. Giving an example or being clear about what success looks like shows kids where they are headed. Sometimes in conferences I share various ways to negotiate the difficulty, a plan or a strategy to keep moving forward. Giving disengaged learners options empowers them. Often, "Here's what I've tried in this situation to get unstuck. What do you want to do?" is enough to get kids back on task. Letting them in on "teacher secrets" builds trust and increases emotional engagement.

3. *Success breeds success.* Students who have experienced a lot of failure tend to check out. Some older students may give up hope that they can do the work their peers do. Sadly, sometimes their teachers have given up on them too. For kids like this, I break the task down into smaller parts so they can taste success and remember how good it feels. I reassure them that I'm looking for thinking, not one right answer. I ask if they are up for a challenge and then quantify what I want them to attempt, perhaps a task as simple as, "Write three pieces of thinking in the form of annotations." (I might add, "If you can do five that's even better.") Annotations help me see who is stuck and who needs a more challenging task. I respond quickly, in writing, underneath. The following class period, I give them verbal feedback in front of their peers: "Wow, Omar, you wrote a question yesterday that I'm still thinking about. You should share that with your group and see what they think." The point is to label what students did well, and suggest they have something important to say. Other ways of getting students to articulate their process so that we can identify their successes and scaffold them through difficulty include:

- In math: ask students to write or talk through the steps of their problem-solving.
- In science: add a section to a lab report in which students articulate what went well and what didn't go well.
- In social studies: give students a chance to discuss what they think they know about a topic before the unit begins. This helps us address biases or misinformation about history and/or cultures. Talk is an essential tool by which students shape and articulate their thinking. It also helps us recognize their strengths and needs.

4. *I'm not the only teacher in the room.* I love it when my students like me; every teacher does. The sense that I'm making a difference feels good. I can count on these students to complete tasks because they want to please me. But being a teacher everyone likes isn't enough. Cajoling a lot of learners into doing what I want doesn't mean students are learning. And there are always students every year who, no matter how nice I am, still don't like me. It's never very many, maybe one or two, usually girls whom I unintentionally annoy. Trying to connect with them burns me out. When I remember that I'm not the only one in the room kids can connect with, my job gets a lot easier. Making it clear that there are many teachers in the room tells students that we need one another to get smarter.

I work hard to build relationships with students, but I can't stop there. I try to create a safe environment where students trust their peers, themselves, and me enough to take risks. I want them to know that everyone's thinking needs to be on the table if we are all to learn. To help learners connect with one another, I plan units that connect with students' hearts, their world, and their interests. I model that everyone's thinking matters. I devote class time to juicy discussions and rarely ask questions that have only one right answer. I encourage collaboration and create opportunities for students to share their "story." The power of story helps kids view their classmates more expansively and empathically, fosters a more open mind-set—the kid with bad grades can have good ideas, just the A student has struggles in other areas. Collaborating with others—students, teachers, and community members—helps students learn more deeply. They learn to be patient with difference and realize they can learn from others. Figure 3–3 lists some guidelines for successful collaboration.

Figure 3–3 Guidelines for Successful Small-Group Collaboration

1. Make sure the task or topic is worth the time. No one wants to talk about something that's already been figured out or work on something that's already been done.

2. Give students a way to hold their thinking before, during, and after the session. My students keep their in-progress work in folders that include (often on sticky notes) questions, confusions, comments, and ideas they want to share with the group.

3, Before the groups meet, brainstorm ways to handle sticky situations. What do group members do when one member talks all the time? Conversely, how do they give quiet teammates a chance to get their voices heard? What happens when group members don't do their share of the work?

4. Let students have some say in how the groups will be constructed. I take more risks when there are people in my group I trust. I also push myself when I'm in groups that I don't know well. Flexible grouping can be a bonus.

5. Be clear about the group's purpose. Explain what is supposed to be accomplished.

I can improve this sense of well-being by honoring risk taking, scaffolding student learning, and helping them see how the work they do in the classroom connects to the world outside of school. I model how I recover from failed attempts and show students how to have respectful discourse when they work with someone who makes a mistake or has a difference of opinion.

We've discussed students' relationship with their teacher and peers, but there's a third, essential piece to emotional engagement—ensuring that students care about the topic or unit. Teaching can't just be about covering the standards. We have to show students how the learning will help them create more connections with the people they care about. Remember, emotional engagement means getting to the "heart" of each student. In *Common Core, Unit by Unit*, Cheryl Dobbertin (2013) writes about "frosting the standards cake." I'm happy to connect cake with anything, but the metaphor of cake as the standards, frosting as the yummy stuff that makes the standards too tempting to resist, is a great way of thinking about how we make topics emotionally engaging. We need to plan and instruct so students can meet the standards, but if there isn't something delicious to dig into on the surface, we will lose them before they get there. Units that provoke high emotional engagement have content that is:

- relatable
- connected to an authentic audience and purpose
- community based and/or connected to current events.

Making the academic content relatable requires getting to know my students. Of course I consider grade level and demographics, but I also ferret out their interests. This is hard to do at the beginning of the year, because I don't know them very well. Typically, I start with a topic connected to a social justice issue.

Another way to make content relatable is to choose a question or problem students are wrestling with in their own lives. One year, many of my students were considering enlisting in the military or had already filled out the paperwork and were waiting for their eighteenth birthday to sign on the dotted line. Many could describe the benefits of enlisting, but few could tell me the risks. When I asked what they knew about current U.S. military conflicts, few could tell me anything. I felt it was important that they knew why they would be putting their lives on the line, so we considered the following question: What do I need to know about U.S. military action to guide my decisions as a citizen, such as choosing whether to enlist or how to vote? To help them gather different perspectives, I used a required novel, *The Things They Carried* (O'Brien 2009), to model thinking strategies for negotiating complex text. I also offered lots of nonfiction choices related to current conflicts and historical wars that would help them see patterns in events and text structures. Connecting the novel and factual information on current conflicts with students' decisions to enlist or vote ramped up their emotional engagement.

A unit on immigration created emotional engagement in a class that included many students who had emigrated to the United States. Some were documented, many were not. Students considered the question as political scientists: how can today's United States manage immigration in ways that are fair and legal? We explored the issue through the positions of prominent political figures on undocumented workers and border restrictions. Students researched the various branches of government to see what each could legally do. They connected political candidates' comments to the Constitution and then debated the legality of their promises.

These are not topic-driven units but rather authentic disciplinary questions that provide real purpose and audience for the work students will do. When I planned the immigration unit around a question that political scientists ask themselves, students' stories led us to another disciplinary question: What responsibility should businesses carry for the undocumented immigrants who work for them? Students knew that local construction companies paid their undocumented workers cash under the table. Several students decided to write letters to these companies explaining why this isn't a good idea. They had an emotional reason to write persuasively. They wanted these business owners to understand that these workers have no recourse should they get injured. They have no insurance, no way to ensure fair wages, and no way to save for old age. The students followed an authentic path of

> In Section 2, page 41, Elizabeth defines disciplinary literacy work as "(1) engaging students in the practices of the discipline (e.g., framing a problem, investigating, analyzing data); (2) eliciting and acquiring the necessary knowledge to carry out those practices using content literacy strategies as tools; (3) examining the words, phrases, and discourses that enable disciplinary work; and (4) evaluating why, when, and how disciplinary language and discourses are useful and why, when, and how they are not."

engagement: from awareness of the problem as individuals to a broader understanding of the problem as political scientists to activists who wanted to make the world better for others.

Cognitive Engagement: The Need to Learn

Here my hairstylist comes to mind. Wanting to supplement her income, Danielle attended dental hygiene school. When she was halfway through the program, I asked how things were going. She told me that when she was in high school, she wasn't a very good student. She would take shortcuts and copy from her friends. She didn't see a purpose for doing the work herself. Then she laughed and said, "I can't do that now. I have to know this information forward and backward so I don't panic when I have a real patient."

Danielle had a psychological drive to learn. She wasn't just going to class and doing the assignments for the grade. She had to know the material so well that she could successfully perform a job she cared about. Her cognitive engagement drove her to monitor her understanding. It forced her to study strategically. She revisited the material and asked for help so she could become a dental hygienist.

In Section 2, Elizabeth explains how important it is to create effective and informed people who can "navigate, assess, and respond to the onslaught of new information, ideas, and perspectives" (page 20). Listening to a lecture on a topic isn't enough to ensure that students meet these twenty-first-century demands. Reading and writing aren't skills for language arts class only. Students need a chance to wrestle with big and important ideas that don't have a simple solution or answer. Focusing solely on the standards, we fail to show our students how what they learn gives them power in the world beyond our classroom. Because the context of a lecture is limited, students are less likely to transfer the information to other learning situations.

Planning for cognitive engagement changed my teaching. It gave me the confidence to limit my lecturing, to give up a little control so that my students could construct meaning and engage in critical thinking.

Telling students they need to "cite strong and thorough evidence to support analysis" invites disengagement. However, if students know that being able to cite and analyze evidence gives them a better chance of persuading others to see and accept their point of view, they have a reason to learn and hold on to this skill—they're cognitively engaged.

Asking students to demonstrate their knowledge or skill to an authentic audience also ramps up cognitive engagement. They're not just learning something to pass a test; their investigation or artifact has a real purpose. When a project, proposal, or piece of writing is directed to a member of the larger community, students feel a greater urgency to revise their thinking and rework their presentation. Their learning matters to someone beyond the classroom. Completing worksheets or taking multiple-choice tests doesn't have the same impact.

When my tenth graders wrote letters to local construction companies about their hiring practices, they cited evidence that supported their argument. They were motivated to find, analyze, and use evidence correctly. They gave the task sustained attention and effort because they wanted their position understood and injustice righted.

When I trigger all three types of engagement, I have my best days in the classroom. When kids aren't engaged, I ask myself: Do the students know the behavior of learners? Have I given them a way to emotionally connect with me, their peers, and/or the topic? Is the topic compelling? Have I connected it to meaningful work and time-worthy tasks? Examining the quality of student engagement helps me determine what shifts in instruction I need to make. When kids are off task, there's a reason. Maybe they don't know what I want them to do. Maybe the texts aren't interesting and they don't care about them. Perhaps the topic or unit needs a tighter connection to purpose and audience. Discovering these reasons helps me get more kids engaged, more often. When I only lecture, it's very hard to figure out what kids need day by day. Focusing on engagement, I provide opportunities for my students to work in meaningful ways.

A Model for Generating
Student Engagement

When I ask successful athletic coaches if they talk for an entire practice session, they scoff, "Of course not! Coaches who do that have teams that never win." Successful coaches model or teach something they think will help their athletes perform better. Then the athletes practice while the coaches coach.

And when I ask coaches if they plan what their athletes will do during a practice session, they say, "Of course! If I didn't, it would be chaos." Planning helps them work with individuals and small groups in real time. They can give feedback or re-model a skill. They vary their guidance to meet varied needs.

If we can do this for our athletes, we can also do it for our students. Reading, writing, problem-solving, and discussing require just as much practice as hitting a line drive or making a layup. Learners need the opportunity to "do." Teachers and coaches need to give feedback on that performance. Skiers don't get better at skiing by listening to someone talk about how to ski. Likewise, no one gets better at critical thinking by regurgitating someone else's PowerPoint slides.

However, practice alone can also lead to disengagement. Learning that isn't geared to a bigger event or product is boring. Athletes and students need a chance to use and demonstrate what they've learned. For athletes, this comes in the form of competition. For students, this demonstration can take a variety of forms: a letter to business owners about initiating fairer labor practices, a roundtable discussion in which students and adults with military affiliations (active members, family of veterans) share different perspectives on enlisting, and so on.

In *So What Do They Really Know? Assessment That Informs Teaching and Learning* (Tovani 2011), my colleague Sam Bennett and I called the approach diagrammed in Figure 3–4 *the workshop model*. I now refer to the approach as *the student engagement model*. My goal is to get more students engaged more often.

Figure 3–4 The Student Engagement Model

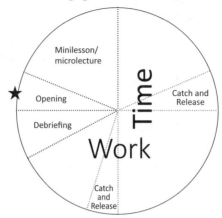

The model's components are:

- *Opening.* I begin planning by setting learning targets. I decide what I want students to know and be able to do by the end of the class, week, and unit. During the opening, I share these daily targets with students. I want them to be clear about the learning goal and what they will create to show me what they know and need. Next, I consider what students will do during their work sessions. How will they meet the targets? What will they read, write, solve, research, and discuss to meet the long-term targets at the end of the unit?

- *Minilesson/microlecture.* Based on student needs I've noted the previous day, I model or teach something to the whole class that will help them continue working independently.

- *Working/thinking session.* Students spend the bulk of their time applying what they are learning. While they are working, I'm still teaching but not the whole class. I differentiate my instruction by conferring with individuals or working with a small group of kids with a similar need. All the while, I notice what students are doing well and what they might need from me to continue learning.

- *Catch and release.* I might discover that I have to regather the class and quickly model or reteach something to keep them going.

- *Debriefing.* At the end of the cycle, I make sure students have time to debrief their learning. They refer back to the learning targets and share what they figured out and what they need to keep going.

Any component can be an entry point. I often start with the mini-lesson or microlecture but not always. I enter the cycle based on students' needs at the end of the previous class period. Approaching the model in this way, I don't have to follow the circular order in which it is presented. I start with whichever component best meets the needs of my learners that day. As I plan and assess for engagement, I focus on what students will do and what skills and information they need to work longer and more productively. Keeping this model in mind ensures that students spend the bulk of their time practicing critical thinking and creating an authentic product.

In a class period of an hour or more, I can usually present a minilesson/microlecture, give kids time to work, and provide an opportunity for them to reflect on their learning. When class periods are less than an hour, it can take two periods to get through all the components. The point is not to race through the cycle. The point is to give students an opportunity to learn something, apply it, and then reflect on new learning. A two-day cycle might look like this:

- I start day one by having students reflect on and review the learning targets. This usually takes five minutes or so.
- I then provide a twelve- to fifteen-minute minilesson/ microlecture.
- If I have a forty-five-minute class period, that leaves about twenty-five minutes for students to work before the bell rings.
- Day two might start with a two-minute catch and release to review the learning targets or to show some student work produced the day before.

- This is the grounding point for another twenty minutes or so of work. I let kids dig back into their reading, writing, researching, or solving.
- While they work, I confer with individuals or work with a small group.
- Before the bell rings, I leave enough time for kids to debrief their learning. They reflect back on the learning targets and share how their thinking has developed.

The student engagement model is a planning and assessment tool. It's not a rigid, lockstep process to be followed in order. When I talk too long during the minilesson/microlecture, students don't get as much time to work as they need. But the following day, I briefly review the learning targets, remind students of what they were doing the previous class period, and let them get right back to work. Sometimes kids are so engrossed that I don't stop them until the bell rings. The following class period, I do a quick catch and release, explaining how students will reflect and share their work in the debriefing. Sometimes students share individually in their response journals or participate in small discussion groups.

Each component in the model supports students so they can work for extended periods. What's important is that students have a chance to experience all the components on a regular basis.

> In lecture, teachers can make assumptions about students' understanding of the content and what they need to do to learn it, but when we build in metacognition, students take responsibility for their own learning. Notice that learning targets focus on the student's actions, not the teacher's.

Opening: Sharing Learning Targets So Kids Know Where They're Headed

In Section 2, Elizabeth reminds us that people learn more effectively when they monitor their progress and have control of their learning goals.

State and national standards guide what I want students to know and be able to do at the end of a unit. I use these standards to design long-term and nested learning targets—goals I want students to meet by the end of a designated period of time. (See the examples in Figure 3–5.) Learners use these goals to monitor their growth and decide what they need next.

Figure 3–5 Long-Term and Nested Targets and Matched Assessments

Long-Term and Nested Targets	Matched Assessments (What Students Will Create or Discuss to Show What They Know and Need)
Long-term target: *I can articulate the effects of war on individuals and society to create awareness in others.* **CCSS RI.1 Grades 11–12** Cite strong and thorough textual evidence to support analysis of what the text says explicitly as well as inferences drawn from the text, including determining where the text leaves matters uncertain. **CCSS W.1 Grades 11–12** Write arguments to support claims in an analysis of substantive topics or texts, using valid reasoning and relevant and sufficient evidence. Nested target (helps students produce quality work so they can meet the long-term target): *I can embed quotes to support my argument about the effects of war.*	Summative assessment: Students write a historical assessment of a war based on immediate financial and human cost and immediate- and long-term political impact. Formative assessments: • Drafts with embedded quotes • Annotated nonfiction texts: questions, connections, possible quotes to embed • Identification and synthesis of accurate data from a variety of sources

Learning targets are *not* objectives or standards with the words *I can* in front of them. The Common Core State Standards are succinct but complex. I break these standards down into manageable pieces so that students know what they mean. I also model strategies students can use to meet the standards.

When I write targets, I use only one verb per target and try to use the word *to* or *so* to connect the target to a reason for doing the work. Good learning targets give students several ways to show their thinking. They are not a to-do list. However, they are written clearly enough that students can tell me what they need to meet the goal.

Every class period, I review and refer to the learning targets and matched assessments. They help me plan what I want students to know and be able to do. They also help students know what is expected of them. Learning targets aren't tasks but rather goals connected to thinking. Long-term targets can take an entire unit to reach; the nested targets help students work toward and meet the long-term targets.

Learning targets are most useful if students have a way to demonstrate during class what they need to know. Next to my learning targets, I write what students will create or talk about during class to show me how close they are to meeting the target. These matched assessments are evidence of students' thinking. It's what they create or say during the cycle to show me what they know and need. In some cases, this evidence is a writing draft or a few simple annotations. It doesn't have to be fancy. (The appendix contains examples of various ways students can show their thinking.)

Based on these assignments, I plan the minilessons/microlectures I present to help kids meet the targets. For example, when I asked students to write a commentary to send to the local newspaper, I first wrote one myself and quickly discovered how complex the assignment was. There were certain minilessons I needed to plan, and the kids would need several opportunities to revise if I expected high-quality products. Following are a few more examples of learning targets (several may take more than one minilesson/microlecture to achieve):

1. *I can craft an original argument to educate and/or influence an audience.*

   Minilessons/microlectures: Examine what a thesis statement is. Recognize that as we write, sometimes our thesis changes. Point out that in my first draft I initially had several thesis statements. As my knowledge increased and my thinking became clearer, I narrowed it down to one. I had to keep reading and writing to figure out which one I really wanted to argue.

2. *I can use evidence to support my argument.*

   Minilessons/microlectures: Connect evidence to the nonfiction texts students have chosen to read. Model how to verify evidence. Discuss how evidence is sometimes tainted or taken out of context. Discuss how to decide which evidence is valid, reasonable, moving.

3. *I can accurately quote the thinking of experts to strengthen my argument.*

   Minilessons/microlectures: Show students how to embed a quote. Focus not only on the punctuation but also on syntax. Model how to write the sentence that precedes the quote to ground it. Model how to comment on the quote in the sentence that follows.

4. *I can use a mentor text to inspire and influence my writing.*

   Minilessons/microlectures: Examine published commentaries. Notice how authors start and conclude their arguments. Analyze evidence and how it is woven into the piece. Look for embedded stories and notice the difference between commentaries that don't have any narratives.

5. *I can use firsthand experience to encourage my audience to care about my topic.*

   Minilessons/microlectures: Model how to read firsthand accounts of soldiers and how to decide if they fit into the argument.

Figure 3–6 is the learning-target rubric for the commentary assignment, which I generated after I wrote my own commentary. Remembering Rick Stiggins' research on how students improve, I focused on only a few aspects of quality at a time. I gave it to kids the day I assigned the commentary, so they'd know up front what targets they were shooting for.

All students get a chance to meet these targets. I don't modify them for language learners or kids with IEPs (individualized education program). Because some students will need more scaffolding than others, I regularly present minilessons/microlectures that support as many students as possible. There isn't a perfect minilesson/microlecture that will meet the needs of everyone in the class, nor can I deal with everyone's needs during this part of the cycle, but I can address these needs during individual conferences. Sometimes kids surprise me and the minilesson/microlecture I've planned isn't what they need. Learning targets not only give me a marker for getting and giving feedback but also give students something on which to reflect. It's important to post the targets and review them frequently; sometimes learners don't know what they mean. Last semester, one of the targets was *I can embed evidence to support my position.* Miguel, an eleventh grader, told me, "Tovani, I can't hit today's target." When I asked why, he said, "I don't know what *embed* means." Several other students piped up: "Yeah, I don't know what that is either." I quickly replaced the minilesson I had planned for that day with some examples of embedded quotes, modeling how students could use their nonfiction text to find quotes to embed.

This took about twelve minutes, and the students then got to work. Some went to their annotated articles to find quotes. Others returned to their writing to see if they had embedded their quotes correctly. During the debriefing, trios of students shared their embedding work and got feedback from their peers.

Figure 3–6 **Writing Reflection**

Commentary on War: Describe an effect (or effects) of war on individuals and/or society. State your position on the United States' involvement in current foreign affairs. Support your argument with a minimum of three pieces of evidence and leave your reader with a call to action.

Name: _____

Final Commentary Due: _____

Editing as a Courtesy to the Reader:

_____ _____ **10 points:** I can use conventions of language correctly: usage, capitalization, punctuation, and spelling.

_____ _____ **10 points:** I can cite sources and embed quotes correctly.

_____ _____ **10 points:** I can demonstrate revision with attached drafts.

Thinking Behind the Essay:

_____ _____ **10 points:** I can describe an effect (or effects) of war on individuals and/or society.

_____ _____ **20 points:** I can state my position on the United States' current involvement in foreign affairs.

_____ _____ **20 points:** I can embed three pieces of evidence that support my position.

_____ _____ **10 points:** I can use narrative and story to hook my reader.

_____ _____ **10 points:** I can call my reader to action.

Student total: _____ out of 100 points

Teacher total: _____ out of 100 points

Writing Reflection: Here's what I want Mrs. Tovani to know about my writing process.

Minilessons/Microlectures: Helping Students
Meet the Targets

A lecture can play an important role in instruction, but I don't want it to dominate. I limit how much I talk. Minilessons/microlectures are an opportunity to model or share something that will help students stay engaged longer while they are working. I plan to talk for no more than ten or fifteen minutes at a time, taking to heart the research (Medina 2008) that even interested adults have to have a "brain break" after ten or twelve minutes. Lecturing judiciously means the talk is intentional and has a clear purpose. I choose specific teaching points and then ask students to use or practice what I have modeled or demonstrated.

At the beginning of the year, I set a timer for twelve minutes to help me get back into "microlecturing" shape. When the timer goes off, I stop talking and the kids get to work. This may sound rigid, but I know too well how easy it is to get carried away once I start talking. Occasionally I may need a few more minutes after I've silenced the timer. Other times I'm finished before it beeps. I keep my minilessons/microlectures lean, focused, and specific to as many student needs as possible. I consciously and strategically plan how I will use this time (see Figure 3–7).

Figure 3–7 Potential Focuses for Minilessons/Microlectures

- Share something provocative to create curiosity about the topic.
- Model what the thinking or work could look like.
- Teach a skill or strategy that will enable students to work independently longer.
- Expand students' background knowledge of the topic.
- Share how to negotiate complex text by modeling a thinking strategy so students can "see" what's happening in your head as you read, write, and solve.

One way we learn is by making connections between new and known information. I think of my minilessons/microlectures as a strip of Velcro that students can use to connect new reading, writing, and thinking. Lecturing in short, conscious bursts, I intentionally teach or model something specific and then ask students to put what they saw or heard into practice. Sometimes they can use the information to read disciplinary text that will help them uncover content. Other times, they use it to revise disciplinary writing.

During the minilesson/microlecture, my goal is to increase background knowledge, model a process, or revisit a concept to help students broaden their conceptual understanding. I teach students something about the content so they can read, write, and discuss their thinking more deeply when they are working. Often my minilesson/microlecture is determined by observations I've made while students were working the previous day, patterns I've noticed that help me see what they need next.

Work Sessions/Conferences: The Heart of the Student Engagement Model

Learning happens when students have a chance to collaborate, discuss, design, and solve problems with others. Back in the 1960s, McMaster University Medical School in Canada recognized the need to give students an opportunity to learn by solving open-ended problems. They labeled this paradigm shift *problem-based learning*. Heeding the research that teaching didn't equate with telling, professors gave students the opportunity, in collaboration with their peers, to investigate and propose solutions to authentic problems in the field. This role shift from lecturer to facilitator increased student engagement and learning.

It's easy to write this off and say, "Yeah, but these are medical students. Of course this will work." However, educators like Finkle and Torp (1995) studied the work that was happening at McMaster University and considered how it could be used as an instructional model for K–12 students. Their goal was to combine problem-solving strategies with disciplinary knowledge. They recognized that to become proficient at thinking critically, one has to practice critical thinking. To do this requires hands-on learning.

Students need time to work every day. Frequently, this occurs after the minilesson/microlecture, the launching pad for the ideas students now put into practice. The work can take different forms depending on the particular disciplinary question and students' needs—students may collaborate on solving a complex math problem; read and annotate a piece of text so that at the end of the period they can discuss how their thinking about the topic expanded; use a revision strategy from the minilesson/microlecture on a recent draft of writing; practice a reading strategy—there are lots of skills and strategies students can practice.

Sometimes I skip the minilesson/microlecture entirely; I quickly review the learning targets, and students get back to work. My first-period class a couple of years ago started at 7:10 a.m., and many of the students worked evening jobs. Several would stagger in late, so I started the class with a work session and presented the minilesson/microlecture twenty minutes into the period. This seemed to meet everyone's needs better.

I gradually increase the time students spend working. At the beginning of the year, it is unrealistic to think students will be able to work productively for long periods: they're not used to it. Ideally, I want students to work for two-thirds of the class period. While they work, I confer with individuals and work with small groups. Again, this model is based on a cycle; if the class period is only forty-five minutes, it may take two days to get through all the components. It's important not to skimp on the work session: this is where the real learning happens. The more time students have to read, write, and discuss, with my support as tutor or facilitator, the more growth they'll experience.

All parts of the student engagement model should remain fluid and be used to sustain and support student engagement (see Figure 3–8). If time spent working is at the heart of student learning, the other components are the primary arteries:

- The *opening* introduces the learning targets and matched assessments.

Figure 3–8 Student Work Time at the Center

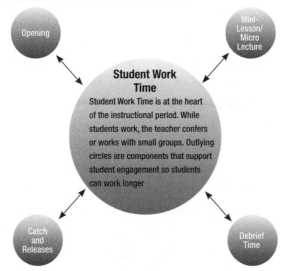

Opening

Mini-Lesson/Micro Lecture

Student Work Time

Student Work Time is at the heart of the instructional period. While students work, the teacher confers or works with small groups. Outlying circles are components that support student engagement so students can work longer

Catch and Releases

Debrief Time

- The *minilesson/microlecture* gives us a chance to model and provide information that students need to continue working independently or in small groups.
- The *catch and release* helps refocus students' learning.
- *Debriefing* allows time for students to reflect on what they've learned and what they need next.

Catch and Release: Refocusing and Reteaching

It's hard to work for long periods without intermittent support. The catch and release, demarcated with dotted lines in Figure 3–4, is a quick timeout to "catch" students when they are stuck. When I notice several students struggling with the same issue, I call the class to attention and quickly teach or model something to get the kids back on track. When students are being introduced to a new topic or learning a new skill, they need more support: there are more catch and releases at the beginning of a unit than at the end. Catch and releases are not always necessary but when they are, they should last no more than a couple of minutes.

Debriefing: Questioning and Reflecting

Debriefing usually takes place at the end of the cycle. This is an opportunity for students to reflect on the day's learning—to synthesize rather than simply retell or summarize. They revisit the learning targets, and I have another chance to probe their thinking. They are accountable to the other learners in the room and to themselves as they talk or write about their learning, reflecting, and assessing the progress they've made.

Sometimes students give me an exit ticket; sometimes they write in their response journals; sometimes they discuss in small groups while I monitor and listen. I record what I notice them doing well, what they need next, and what they say about the content or process that might be important for the whole class to hear.

It's easy to forget the debriefing component of the cycle. Teachers often tell me, "My students were working so well that I didn't want to interrupt." I understand those glorious times when all students are working intently and productively. However, if we regularly skip this component, students begin to think their work doesn't matter. Giving students time to debrief holds all learners accountable, not in a punitive way but in a way that suggests we need everyone's thinking to do our best work.

Evaluating the Use of Instructional Time

Time has been mentioned a lot in this section. My instructional coach, Sam Bennett, helps me remember how quickly time in the classroom speeds by. She visits mine regularly throughout the year and records what I say and what students do. Initially, to keep me honest, she adds up the minutes to see who is doing the majority of the work. After a few of these visits, I start to get into the rhythm of shorter lectures and longer work sessions. I start every year this way because it's too easy for me to fall into the habit of only lecturing.

Recognizing how we use our own time is tough. In my work as a professional developer, I've had the privilege of working with districts over the course of several years. In districts where teachers are given feedback about how they use their time, they often begin lecturing less, and students begin working more.

Brandon Martin, an exemplary principal in Missouri, wanted to help his teachers notice how each minute of a class was spent. On his computer he created a template by drawing a circle, sectioned into the individual minutes in a class period. He then observed classes, indicating how each minute was being used:

- No teaching or learning is happening. (Students are getting their materials, forming groups, chatting while the teacher collects materials, or cleaning up at the end of the period.)
- The teacher is talking while kids listen, or asking questions that individual students answer.
- Students are either reading, writing, solving, discussing, or creating something that represents critical thinking.

Brandon then emailed the time wheels to the respective teachers and asked them to reflect on how they'd used their class time.

Figure 3–9 is the time wheel he completed for a ninth-grade language arts class. During the first three minutes, students picked up their work folders and novels and then formed groups. For the next seven minutes, the teacher modeled how to get unstuck on a problem she noticed several students were having. She quickly gave directions for the final project and sent the kids off to work. While students worked, she monitored and conferred. The last four minutes of class, students returned their materials and got ready for the bell to ring.

Figure 3–10 is the time wheel Brandon completed for a chemistry class. As the students entered the room, they began working on a problem written on the board. After two minutes, the teacher interrupted and collected homework for five minutes. He then had students form groups, which took another four minutes. Student groups then worked for nine minutes on an activity in which they used the periodic table. Then they spent two minutes returning to their regular seats. Next they spent three minutes reading the directions on a handout. For the

Figure 3–9 Time Wheel for Ninth-Grade Language Arts

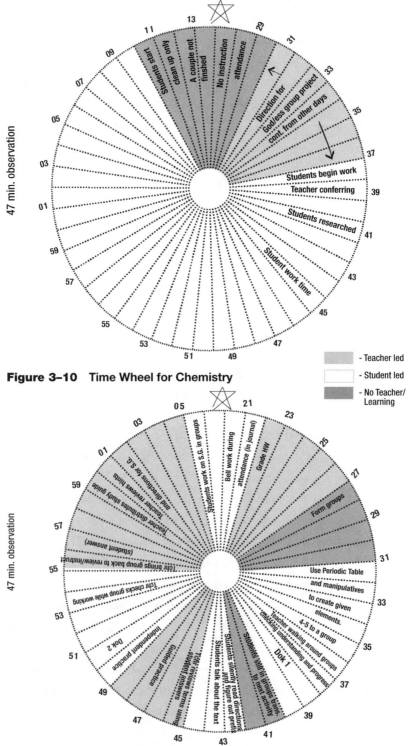

Figure 3–10 Time Wheel for Chemistry

Legend:
- Teacher led
- Student led
- No Teacher/Learning

Figure 3–11 Time Wheel for American Government

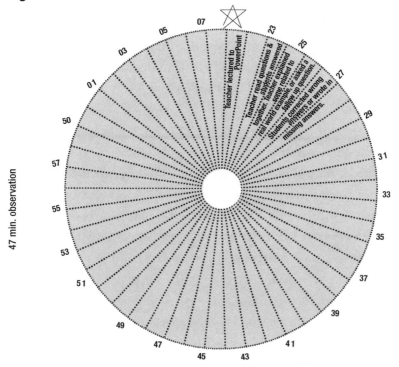

47 min. observation

next four minutes the teacher modeled solving a practice problem. He then gave the students six minutes to solve a problem on their own. After that he spent ten minutes going over the problem. During the last two minutes, students worked on a problem in their textbook. In total, the teacher talked for nineteen minutes, and students worked independently for twenty-two minutes.

The chemistry teacher was surprised to learn that he took five minutes to collect homework and six minutes to get kids in and out of groups, commenting that he "wasted" eleven minutes. Doing a little math, he realized that eleven minutes a day, five days a week, times four weeks a month, is a total of 220 minutes. Together he and Brandon brainstormed other ways to collect homework and arrange groups to get that time back.

Figure 3–11 is the completed time wheel from an American government class. Students got lots of information from a lecture/PowerPoint presentation the teacher delivered but had no time to process it. When

Brandon asked this teacher what the students had taken away from the presentation, he said, "I won't know until they take the test," which was two weeks away. When asked what he does about the students who don't pass the test, he said, "I have got to keep going. I have too much content to slow down."

I understand this teacher's urgency. This will be the last time many of these students will take an American government class (and based on the current state of politics in the United States, our citizenry could use a little more knowledge about the way our government works). Unfortunately, hearing content doesn't ensure learning content.

According to a May 31, 2016, blog post from eLearning Infographics, the number-one way to become a twenty-first-century educator is to shun memorizing. It ominously warns, "If educators allow teaching to exist mostly as delivering information that students memorize, their job descriptions could be quickly outsourced to Google!" Often the purpose of lecturing is to increase students' background knowledge. If students only spit back the information on a test and never get a chance to think critically, Google might as well take over.

The North Kansas City school district, where I've also had the privilege of working for several years, hires literacy and numeracy experts from around the county, as well as from within the district, to provide high-quality professional development. The common denominator for the goals of this teacher training is creating classrooms in which students spend the majority of their time working. Recently, administrators there shared some very simple but impressive data comparing students who were getting more time to work than time to listen with students in lecture-based classrooms. Their test scores on state and district assessments were revelatory. In classes where students were getting more time to read, write, and engage in critical thinking, scores on high-stakes assessments went up. (See Figure 3–12.)

Figure 3–12 tells another piece of the assessment story. It takes the same academic achievement results and slices them differently, specifically comparing cohort versus noncohort teachers. We wanted to see what

Figure 3–12 North Kansas City School District Comparison of Effects of Lecture-Only Classes to Increased Student Work Time Classes on Student Performance (MAP = Missouri Assessment Program; EOC = End-of-Course Exams)

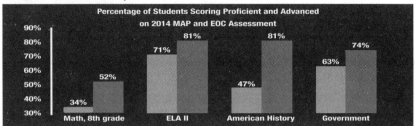

happens when you have the applied effect. Left-hand columns represent students of teachers who have not participated in one of our cohort learning opportunities; right-hand columns represent students of teachers who have. The results are very clear—compared with their peers, students of teachers who are directly involved in professional development cohorts (all of whom structure time so students get the majority of class time to read, write, and discuss) on average score better on state assessments.

It's natural to want to share all we know with students. We are experts in our content and subject matter. But there is no way to share all we know in a semester or even a year. Students don't need all my knowledge to practice and improve their critical thinking skills. I want to harness students' thinking so that they are able to use the content of the course to construct meaning. A little knowledge can go a long way.

Problem-Based Learning: Daily Work Matters

Without long-term lesson planning, the student engagement model is difficult to sustain. Long-term planning makes daily reading, writing, solving, and thinking possible because it harnesses the power of purpose and audience. Creating something that others will consume or working to solve a problem that hasn't already been solved gives students a reason to read, write, and discuss. When there is real work to be done, students are prompted to research, argue, read, and synthesize. Letting students "do the discipline" means giving them a chance to engage in activities that scientists, mathematicians, historians, social scientists, and literary critics pursue. It also means giving students the opportunity to create products related to those fields.

Several years ago, a teacher told me she wasn't a historian, just a social studies teacher. Her comment not only diminished her importance as a teacher but also denied the real-world application of her content. I pushed her to consider how she could use class time to prepare students to do the important work associated with social studies disciplines like anthropology, geography, history, economics, political science, and sociology.

In Section 2, Elizabeth explains the value of "problem-solving experiences that help students develop increasingly specialized concepts and language." Problem-based learning starts with student-centered planning. Learners need an opportunity to explore a subject or content area by solving an open-ended problem. They develop their content knowledge and practice the strategies that will help them become better critical thinkers. Planning for problem-based learning starts with a framed problem or driving question that invites discovery. The work that students do has a real-world connection; it's shared with more than the classroom teacher in a format that exists in the world outside school. No more book reports or dioramas that sit on a shelf in the library. Completing the work requires that students interact with classmates and the community, not just their teacher.

Problem-based learners also use technology and a variety of texts to increase their background knowledge. They don't rely solely on us for their information. As students work, they connect new knowledge to what they already know. They have opportunities to draft and revise their thinking, collect and analyze data, evaluate different perspectives, and investigate case studies to help them compare and contrast the present with the past. They do more than "one and done" activities.

Problem-based learning asks students to work on something that doesn't have a ready-made solution. Instead of telling students what they need to know, we give them opportunities to ask questions and solve real problems using the tools and processes of scientists, historians, mathematicians, engineers, activists, social scientists, artists, and musicians. Some examples of problem-based learning are presented in Figure 3–13.

Figure 3–13 Examples of Problem-Based Learning

Discipline or Content-Area Topic/Standard	Real-World Problem Students Can Solve/ Product They Can Create to Demonstrate Their Understanding
Common Core Standards Quantities: CCSS.MATH.CONTENT.HSN.Q.A.1 CCSS.MATH.CONTENT.HSN.Q.A.2 CCSS.MATH.CONTENT.HSN.Q.A.3 Reason quantitatively and use units to solve problems. CCSS.MATH.CONTENT.HSN.Q.A.1 Use units as a way to understand problems and to guide the solution of multistep problems; choose and interpret units consistently in formulas; choose and interpret the scale and the origin in graphs and data displays. CCSS.MATH.CONTENT.HSN.Q.A.2 Define appropriate quantities for the purpose of descriptive modeling. Writing: CCSS.ELA-LITERACY.W.9-10.1 Write arguments to support claims in an analysis of substantive topics or texts, using valid reasoning and relevant and sufficient evidence.	How can we better understand the financial reality of American families? With a small group of peers, choose two families at different socioeconomic levels to evaluate. Review income, planned monthly and annual expenditures, and common unexpected expenditures for a family of four. Create a budget that feels realistic based on this. Identify potential stress points for that family. Based on the budget and stress points, what advice would you give that family? What information do you think would be helpful for politicians/decision makers to know about this family's financial situation? This project will be part of an ongoing question in mathematics: how can we use the tools and processes of math to understand authentic problems and present solutions?

(continues)

(continued)

National Curriculum Standards for Social Studies

Subject area: U.S. history

Level: secondary/high school

Historical period: civil rights; social education

Common Core Standards

Presentation of Knowledge and Ideas:

CCSS.ELA-LITERACY.SL.9-10.4

Present information, findings, and supporting evidence clearly, concisely, and logically such that listeners can follow the line of reasoning and the organization, development, substance, and style are appropriate to purpose, audience, and task.

How can a speech, given at one moment in time, capture an important struggle in American life and imagine a positive way forward? How can we use those speeches as mentors for the present?

At the beginning of the year, students will choose from a collection of speeches addressing social and economic rights in the United States. Students will inquire into the craft of the speech, both its construction and delivery, and the historical context, audience, and speaker's purpose. Over the course of two weeks, small groups of students will lead discussions of each speech with whole-group consideration of the civil rights issues and different approaches that have emerged in U.S. history. Students will choose a contemporary civil rights issue that they care about. They will write and deliver a public speech on this issue at the time we cover one of their mentor speechwriters in our sequential study of history. This speech will be part of an ongoing reflection on the value of knowing our history: how can we use the tools and understandings of the past to help us make sense of the present?

(continues)

Common Core Standards	How is reading part of our social identities?
Craft and Structure:	As part of students' ongoing choice-based reading, they will create reading lists for teenagers (models include the teenreads website (www.teenreads.com), Jon Scieszka's guysread website (www.guysreads.com), and *My Ideal Bookshelf Collection*) as well as book reviews and book talks. Students will choose the categories of their reading lists and consider how well these lists serve their peers and their own reading lives. Students will consider the idiosyncrasies of a reading life, how people respond to persuasion, and how talking, reading, and writing about what we read can feed our reading lives in positive ways.
CCSS.ELA-LITERACY.CCRA.R.4	
Interpret words and phrases as they are used in a text, including determining technical, connotative, and figurative meanings, and analyze how specific word choices shape meaning or tone.	
CCSS.ELA-LITERACY.CCRA.R.5	
Analyze the structure of texts, including how specific sentences, paragraphs, and larger portions of the text (e.g., a section, chapter, scene, or stanza) relate to each other and the whole.	
CCSS.ELA-LITERACY.CCRA.R.6	
Assess how point of view or purpose shapes the content and style of a text.	
Integration of Knowledge and Ideas:	
CCSS.ELA-LITERACY.CCRA.R.7	
Integrate and evaluate content presented in diverse media and formats, including visually and quantitatively, as well as in words.	
Range of Reading and Level of Text Complexity:	
CCSS.ELA-LITERACY.CCRA.R.10	
Read and comprehend complex literary and informational texts independently and proficiently.	

(continues)

(continued)

Next Generation Science Standards

Mendelian genetics

Common Core Standards

Range of Reading and Level of Text Complexity:

CCSS.ELA-LITERACY.RST.9-10.10

By the end of grade 10, read and comprehend science/technical texts in the grades 9–10 text complexity band independently and proficiently.

Integration of Knowledge and Ideas:

CCSS.ELA-LITERACY.RST.9-10.7

Translate quantitative or technical information expressed in words in a text into visual form (e.g., a table or chart) and translate information expressed visually or mathematically (e.g., in an equation) into words.

Presentation of Knowledge and Ideas:

CCSS.ELA-LITERACY.SL.9-10.4

Present information, findings, and supporting evidence clearly, concisely, and logically such that listeners can follow the line of reasoning and the organization, development, substance, and style are appropriate to purpose, audience, and task.

Writing:

CCSS.ELA-LITERACY.W.9-10.2

Write informative/explanatory texts to examine and convey complex ideas, concepts, and information clearly and accurately through the effective selection, organization, and analysis of content.

How can we communicate our knowledge of science in ways that help others?

In small groups, students will research a specific disease and current treatment options. They will then consider how to apply that information to a hypothetical patient and role-play the conversation between the doctor and the patient and his or her loved ones. Students will reflect on the challenges inherent in this task.

Problem-Based Learning in the English Language Arts

In a typical language arts classroom, students alternate a class period spent reading a section of an assigned novel and answering questions about it with one in which the teacher lectures on and recaps the previous day's reading. The final project is an essay that only the teacher will read. The unit culminates in a test.

Here's an alternative.

In a nine-week unit, my junior English class considers what students needed to know about U.S. military action to guide their decisions as a citizen, such as choosing whether to enlist. We use *The Things They Carried*, by Tim O'Brien (2009), as an anchor text to provide a common experience. I model thinking strategies for students that will help them make sense of this complex text. Students have opportunities to read and discuss sections of the book that help them meet state and national standards. (I refer back to this work throughout the year so students can compare and contrast their thinking about the writer's craft relative to other works they read.) Optional text choices come into the mix through nonfiction. Students have many opportunities to increase their background knowledge about the setting of the novel (Vietnam), as well as about current wars and conflicts the United States is involved in. They also read commentaries by liberal, conservative, and moderate historians and contemporary journalists.

Students use thinking strategies to understand a complex literary work. They write a commentary stating their position on current U.S. conflicts, and they design an infographic to hold and organize information they've learned about Vietnam, the Middle East, and modern terrorism. To show their understanding, students take a test on the anchor novel, submit the final draft of their commentary to a local newspaper, and use the infographic as part of a military roundtable discussion (a lunch with twenty-five invited guests who have or had a stake in the military: active and retired soldiers and officers, mothers, social workers). Everything that I model or that the students read (the novel, historical nonfiction, and current essays) and write is directed toward preparing them for this real-world discussion.

During the roundtable, soldiers with post-traumatic stress disorder comment on their struggles; officers discuss their duties; mothers share emotions ranging from sadness to pride as they speak of their children's service. Students share their perspectives as well. They ask questions, increase their background knowledge, and share what they learned over the course of the unit.

Students have a variety of options during the daily work sessions: read the novel, work on their commentary, revise their infographic based on new articles they've read. As students are working, I confer with individuals and help small groups explore a topic more deeply. Each mini-lesson/microlecture is related to something students need to complete in preparation for the military roundtable.

At the end of the unit, students can better articulate the effects of war on individuals and society. Students who considered enlisting before this unit of study have learned that enlisting has risks, not just rewards. They better understand current instances of international terrorism and the issues connected to foreign policy.

We all have required curriculum and need to show why our content matters. When I taught eleventh graders who were mostly Latino and African American students from economically stressed homes, I was challenged: why did they need to read *The Great Gatsby*? Why should they care about some rich white guy? I decided to flip the American Dream idea on its head and consider its dark side—sometimes Americans will stop at nothing to get what they want. The protagonist, Jay Gatz, gave up a great deal to achieve his dream. I posed provocative questions: How much are they willing to give up for their dream? What are they willing to risk to get it? Is the American Dream still possible for teens today? They thought about this as authors of fiction like F. Scott Fitzgerald do, by considering how characters can represent ideas and questions, and they considered it as political scientists do, by evaluating the economic conditions and opportunities of today's diverse citizens, and as historians do, by considering the economic conditions and opportunities during the time F. Scott Fitzgerald wrote his novel. But they do more than report—they synthesize answers to these questions as writers, literary critics, political scientists, and historians. As teachers who do problem-based teaching, we give students the authority of these disciplines rather than subjugate them to the authority of others' past work.

Because the only way I can tell whether students are cognitively engaged is by what they say or create, I give students time to record their thinking and discuss it with their peers. Often during the debriefing sessions, small groups of students share how their thinking has deepened. They discuss new ideas about the guiding questions. They share annotations and quotations from their reading. They read portions of their writing and ask for feedback.

Once I've come up with a compelling connection and a few open-ended questions, I think about what I want students to know and be able to do. For them to demonstrate that they've learned, they need an authentic problem to solve at the end of the unit and they need a way to share that with someone besides me. What students create helps me see whether they are cognitively engaged. Because I can't wait until the end of the unit to find this out, I also give students daily opportunities to leave tracks of their thinking. This helps me adjust my long-term plan and my daily instruction. No assignment can live in isolation. Each one should be directed toward the final product and the summative assessments at the end of the unit.

One of the end products for my juniors who read *Gatsby* was to a write a dream speech. I asked them to describe their dream, explain what the challenges were in obtaining it, and identify what they do or give up to realize it. They had to create awareness in others, inspire an audience of their choosing to believe in their dream as well. Knowing the end product to which my instruction is leading streamlines my planning. These students needed models for their writing. They needed to increase their background knowledge about both the historical setting of *The Great Gatsby* and current economic events to be able to take and support a position on the possibility of achieving the American Dream. I offered a variety of nonfiction texts to choose from: speeches by Martin Luther

King Jr., Maya Angelou, Anna Quindlen, past presidents, and others. They investigated the writer's craft to learn how great speechwriters capture the attention of their audience and use literary techniques to convey meaning. Periodicals, newspapers, and historical texts increased their background knowledge about the twenties and current events, as well as showed how arguments can be crafted.

When students have a real audience with whom to share their work, they are more invested in their learning. Having a wider audience than just me impels my students to improve the quality of their work. Close reading now has a purpose. I don't have to cajole them to revise. When students work with a personal purpose, they work harder; engagement soars.

My *Gatsby* juniors decided who the audience for their dream speech would be:

- Fernando wrote to local legislatures about his dream to earn citizenship. He explained that immigrants aren't illegally crossing the Mexican border to break the law but to get away from drug dealers and a devastated economy. He passionately argued that "his people" just want to find a place to live where their families can be safe and work hard. Fernando loves the United States so much that he plans to serve in the military as a way of "paying back" this country for the life it has given him.

- Ebony wrote about her learning disability; she dreams of a time when people will judge her by her accomplishments, not her test scores. Her target audience was younger students in the school's special education classrooms. She wanted them to believe in themselves more than they believe in their test scores.

- Omar wrote his speech for his parents. He wanted to help them understand more about American teenagers and his struggle to fit in. He told them how hard it is to be a Pakistani teen in America. He shared his speech at the dinner table, hoping to convince them to let him spend a little less time doing homework so that he can play on the lacrosse team. His dream is to blend in a little more, be like other kids his age.

Following are two more examples of discipline-specific problems my students have tackled. Each unit has an anchor text the whole class gets to experience. This text allows me to model specific reading and writing strategies, skills, and processes. Every student is exposed to it in some way. Some read it in its entirety; others read portions of it while I summarize the parts they aren't able to get to or that are too difficult. Students with IEPs who have conditions that prevent them from reading, and newly arrived English language learners, use listening devices. There are also optional reading choices that support the theme.

Why is being an adolescent so difficult and can literature help?

Anchor Text: *The Catcher in the Rye*

Disciplines: Fiction writing, literary criticism, psychology

Optional Reading Choices: Nonfiction information about defense mechanisms, research on history of slang, research on adolescence, autobiographical information about the author, diverse responses (journalism and literary analysis) to *The Catcher in the Rye*

Project and Audience: Give "goodreads" recommendations why tenth graders should (or shouldn't) read *The Catcher in the Rye*; develop recommended book lists for adolescents.

Slavery still exists. How can we help end human trafficking?

Anchor Text: Selected contemporary news media articles on modern-day slavery

Disciplines: Journalism, civil rights activism, economics, fine arts

Optional Reading Choices: *Iqbal, Crossing the Wire, Sacred Leaf, Day of Tears*

Project and Audience: Write op-ed pieces and/or open letters to politicians /companies that offer specific calls to action on ending slavery.

Problem-Based Learning Guidelines

I rarely create units lasting less than four weeks. If something isn't worth digging into for at least that long, it may not be worth students' time. When I look closely at short units, I usually discover they don't have a context and focus on skills that could be embedded in a larger unit. For example, I could teach a grammar unit in three weeks, but because it doesn't have any context, student writing doesn't get better. Instead of reeling off grammar rules and having kids complete worksheets, I embed the rules in the writing projects students undertake during the year.

Units of study need to connect to the standards and to something that matters outside the classroom. I push myself to explain how the unit will make students better human beings ten years from now. I imagine the most disengaged student in the world asking, "Why do I have to learn this?" I want to have an answer ready. If I do, I am well on the way to engaging students cognitively. Without a vision, it's difficult to sift and sort the texts I'll use, the standards I'll teach toward, and the work students will produce to show me they've met the learning targets. If I'm not clear where we're headed, the kids won't be either. When I plan for the long term, I ask myself:

- How can I connect my content to the world outside school?
- Why should my students care about this? What real problem will they be attempting to solve?
- What will they create? Is it something that exists in the real world? Which disciplines will they be relying on to solve this problem?
- Who will hear or see their work besides me?

Content needs context. For classes in reading intervention, social studies, or English language arts, I can easily connect an important question about a hot topic or current event to a theme or time period and build a unit around that. In math or science it gets a little trickier.

While watching the latest NASA achievement the other night, I said to my husband, "If I taught physics or math, I'd use this space probe to ask my students to address some of the problems inherent in this task as engineers, physicists, and computer scientists." We sometimes fall into the trap of thinking we have to teach kids all the "facts" before they can think about the important stuff. Unfortunately, being inundated by all these facts can easily cause a student to disengage.

I've worked with many talented teachers who have made their facts relatable to kids. Matt and Danielle, science teachers in Blue Springs, Missouri, took their genetic unit to another level by using a cystic fibrosis case study to help students see why genetic counseling is important. As a final product, students created a script for counseling parents, complete with Punnett squares, charts, and other information explaining possible risks. As students worked on their final projects, they asked better questions, identified their confusions, and drew conclusions about the information they learned in class. Within this context, alleles, protein synthesis, and DNA mutations had a lot more meaning.

When I look at problem-based units like these, I consider all the possible identities we're offering students and realize that not doing this work means not offering students these possibilities. When we don't let children learn how to solve problems as mathematicians, historians, journalists, civil rights activists, or artists in our classrooms today, we are communicating that we don't believe they will be that tomorrow. And that's not what we mean.

The Marriage of Long-Term and Daily Planning

Each component of the student engagement model fortifies the work the students are doing and gives them the stamina and information they need to keep at it. I focus on determining what students need each day to keep them engaged in critical thinking. I listen to and observe students to learn what they need next.

Thinking back on thirty-three years of teaching, I know there was never a day when every student was engaged for every minute of every class. Principals sometimes chide teachers for this and give them demerits for off-task student behavior. By the same token, I've never been to a staff meeting at which every teacher was 100 percent engaged for every minute. No one can stay continuously engaged. But when we plan for students' behavioral, emotional, and cognitive engagement, more learning happens for more students than if we only lecture.

My favorite teaching days are those on which I feel a palpable hum in the classroom. Students are working independently on work that matters to them. They are far from silent—murmurs abound and sometimes an excited voice rises above the buzz. Looking up from a conference, I see students reading, writing, and discussing. On these days, I see by the work students produce and hear by the comments they make that they are engaged. I have evidence that critical thinking is taking place. This "real work" doesn't just happen. It has to be planned long before the students get to class.

Why go to the effort of planning so kids can read, write, and think when planning a lecture is so much easier? Here's one reason.

Late in June, a couple of weeks after the school year ended, I got an email from Fernando:

Dear Ms. Tovani, I know it is too late to get more points for this, but I've been working on my dream speech and I wanted you to have a copy of it in case you get a chance to share it with someone who can make a difference. All my best wishes, Fernando

The revised dream speech was attached. The due date for this assignment had been back in May, but Fernando kept working on his speech. The previous version had been mailed to the local Colorado legislature, because sharing it in person could have jeopardized his family. Rereading it, I reflected on how much he had grown as a reader, writer, and thinker. This fifth revision, which he did on his own, showed how much he had learned—how many minilessons/microlectures had sunk in and how valuable time to work had been.

Fernando's first line introduces a beautiful simile that he then weaves throughout the speech: "Immigrants are like the common nighthawk, migrating to a better place." Throughout the speech, he compares immigrants to this nocturnal, camouflaged bird most distinguishable by the beautiful song it sings. I think about the undocumented students I've taught—how they sink seamlessly into the shadows when trying to survive, but when they are given the chance to be part of a community, the "song" they sing can be exquisite.

The spelling and grammar in some parts of the speech still need work, but Fernando knows that when describing his journey across the Sonoran Desert at age four, in the special shoes his father had sent from the North, he can't use just any noun or verb: "What made me feel safe, were the shoes my dad gave me, the shoes that lit up with every step I took. But they were more than just shoes. I cherished them because they gave me a feeling that my dad was with me at all times guiding my every step."

Fernando has learned that stories can move readers to action. He describes the "coyote" (the man guiding the family to the border) sprinting toward him with panic in his eyes. He conjures the sharp knife the coyote uses to cut out the blinking soles. When that doesn't work, "He had to throw away my precious shoes." Ignoring his four-year-old feet bloodied from crossing, he ends the paragraph with, "It felt as if I were leaving my dad behind."

Fernando initially wrote this speech for a grade. But he continued to improve it because he saw how his writing could make a difference. He learned the power of being literate. Fernando was not a newly arrived immigrant. But for years he struggled to read and write well in English. Was it because he took on the fashion of a tough guy and tried to hide his poor skills by looking intimidating? Did his teachers give up on him? Was he mostly in classes where the teacher did the majority of work? I don't know.

I do know that the student engagement model helped me help him. If I had lectured all period, every day, I would have missed Fernando. But after a few short work-sessions and conferences, I knew that below the surface of that tough exterior was a kindhearted teenager who wanted to be an American more than anything in the world.

His speech concludes:

> It has been thirteen years since I first migrated to the United
> States and the only thing that hasn't changed is my hope. My
> hope to live like a normal American. My hope to go to college.
> My hope to enjoy the freedom of this country without the fear of
> being deported. My hope to become a Marine and be the shield
> and guardian of this nation's freedom. Even though I wasn't born
> in the United States, I am American. Let us spread our wings and
> feel the freedom. Immigrants are like the nighthawk migrating to
> a better place in search of a better tomorrow.

His repetition of his first line in his last wraps the speech up with a beautiful bow. I can't help thinking that if those thirteen years in the United States had been spent doing instead of listening, Fernando would write and read better than I do.

When I limit my lectures and plan for kids to do the work, more students stay engaged, some after the school year is over. When student engagement increases, so does learning. When we align our practices with our beliefs and support those practices with the work of researchers, we can better meet the demands of the next generation.

AFTERWORD

NELL K. DUKE

A few years ago, veteran teacher Alexis Wiggins spent two days shadowing a high-school student and reflected on her experience in a blog post (Wiggins 2014a, 2014b). Among her key takeaways is that high school students "are sitting passively and listening during approximately 90% of their classes." As an early childhood educator, this statistic gave me heart palpitations. We would never dream of recommending this proportion of listening to speaking or doing over the course of a young child's day. I know that high school students are different—but they're not *that* different.

In this book, you have learned about a variety of alternatives to students sitting passively and listening—and about research behind many of these approaches. Importantly, both authors have taken care to point out that there are times when it is appropriate for the teacher to tell and the students to listen (though never passively, we hope). It's really a matter of telling when the time is right and employing other instructional strategies that, in concert with telling, will result in optimal learning for students.

To choose among the rich repertoire of instructional strategies referenced in this book, you'll need to invoke the practice of beginning with the end in mind: *What do I want students to know or be able to do? How will I know whether students know or are able to do this?* Your goals, and what it looks like for students to have met them, drive our instructional decisions. From there, you'll want to ask: *What do I know about my learners in relation to these goals?* Perhaps you know that some of your students already know or are able to do this. Perhaps you know that the family of one of your students has a personal connection to the topic at hand that you could capitalize upon. Perhaps you know that current distractions in the lives of some of your students will mean you'll need to provide particular support for engagement in this material. Next, you can consider *What are the texts and other tools available to support students' learning? Videos? Artifacts? Articles? Objects?* And so on. At this point, you'll be primed to identify or generate instructional strategies that are likely to be most engaging and effective. Of course, this process is much easier said than done, but I believe that Cris and Elizabeth have provided much information that can facilitate it.

I have a high school student and a soon-to-be middle school student myself. My hope for them, and for all students, is that school will not be 90 percent sitting passively and listening. I am so appreciative to you for taking the time to engage with this book in relation to your practice, and to Cris and Elizabeth for providing the resource. Together, we can change teaching and learning for the better.

APPENDIX

Sample Text Set Guide Sheet

Title of Text Set: _____

Name: _____

Please complete the following tasks as you preview your text set:

1. Read one piece of text and answer the following questions:

Title:

Description of the piece:

One memorable aspect of the text:

2. Choose two other texts that look different from your first choice:

Title:

Topic:

Title:

Topic:

3. Write a letter to me addressing the following questions:

    a. What is your opinion of the contents of this text set?

    b. What should be added to make this text set better?

    c. How might you use this text set in U.S. history?

SILENT READING RESPONSE SHEET

Name: _____

Hour: _____

Title: _____

Page _____ to page _____

While you are reading today, complete #1:

1. On the back of the page, share your thinking about what you read. You may want to tell about a confusing part and then try to ask a question that will isolate the confusion. Maybe you want to ask a question about something that you are just curious about. Share a line that strikes you or a personal connection that you make to the reading. Feel free to give your opinion or your assessment of the reading material. Your response should be at least five sentences long.

Before the class ends, spend five to ten minutes jotting down what you remember about today's reading. Try to write something that will jog your memory and help you remember where you left off. Stretch yourself to write more than you did the last time you did this sheet.

2. I remember reading today about:

DOUBLE-STRATEGY, DOUBLE-ENTRY DIARY

Name: _____

Quote from article	Connection to quote

Quote or word from article	Question

HIGHLIGHT AND REVISIT

Quote highlighted (record words from text)	Reason for highlighting	New or deeper thinking

REFERENCES

Alexander, P. A. 1998. "The Nature of Disciplinary and Domain Learning: The Knowledge, Interest, and Strategic Dimensions of Learning from Subject-Matter Text." In *Learning from Text Across Conceptual Domains*, edited by C. Hynd, 263–87. Mahwah, NJ: Lawrence Erlbaum Associates.

Alexander, P. A., and T. L. Jetton. 2000. "Learning from Text: A Multidimensional and Developmental Perspective." In *Handbook of Reading Research*, edited by M. Kamil, P. D. Pearson, R. Barr, and P. Mosenthal, 285–310. Mahwah, NJ: Lawrence Erlbaum Associates.

Alexander, P. A., and J. E. Judy. 1988. "The Interaction of Domain-Specific and Strategic Knowledge in Academic Performance." *Review of Educational Research* 58(4): 375–404.

Alexander, P. A., J. M. Kulikowich, and S. K. Schulze. 1994. "How Subject-Matter Knowledge Affects Recall and Interest." *American Educational Research Journal* 31 (2): 313–37.

Alozie, N. M., E. B. Moje, and J. S. Krajcik. 2010. "An Analysis of the Supports and Constraints for Scientific Discussion in High School Project-Based Science." *Science Education* 94 (3): 395–427.

Anderson, R. C., and P. D. Pearson. 1984. "A Schema-Theoretic View of Basic Processes in Reading Comprehension." In *Handbook of Reading Research*, Vol. II, edited by P. D. Pearson, R. Barr, M. L. Kamil, and P. Mosenthal, 225–53. New York: Longman.

Anyon, J. 1981. "Social Class and School Knowledge." *Curriculum Inquiry* 11 (1): 3–42.

Bain, R. B. 2005. "'They Thought the World Was Flat?' HPL Principles in Teaching High School History." In *How Students Learn: History, Mathematics, and Science in the Classroom*, edited by J. Bransford and S. Donovan, 179–214. Washington, DC: National Academies Press.

Bass, H. 2006. "What Is the Role of Oral and Written Language in Knowledge Generation in Mathematics?" Paper presented at the Adolescent Literacy Symposium, March 6. University of Michigan, Ann Arbor, MI.

Berrett, D. 2012. "Harvard Conference Seeks to Jolt University Teaching." *The Chronicle of Higher Education*, February 5.

Blumenfeld, P., E. Soloway, R. Marx, J. S. Krajcik, M. Guzdial, and A. S. Palincsar. 1991. "Motivating Project-Based Learning: Sustaining the Doing, Supporting the Learning." *Educational Psychologist* 26 (3–4): 369–98.

Bransford, J., ed. 2000. *How People Learn*. Washington, DC: National Academies Press.

Bransford, J., and S. Donovan, eds. 2005. *How Students Learn; History, Mathematics, and Science in the Classroom*. Washington, DC: National Academies Press.

Bransford, J. D., L. Zech, D. Schwartz, B. Barron, N. J. Vye, and the Cognition and Technology Group at Vanderbilt. 1998. "Designs for Environments That Invite and Sustain Mathematical Thinking." In *Symbolizing, Communicating, and Mathematizing: Perspectives on Discourse, Tools, and Instructional Design*, edited by P. Cobb. Mahwah, NJ: Lawrence Erlbaum Associates.

Carnegie Council on Advancing Adolescent Literacy. 2010. *Time to Act: An Agenda for Advancing Literacy for College and Career Success*. New York: Carnegie Corporation of New York.

Chappuis, J., R. J. Stiggins, S. Chappuis, and J. A. Arter. 2004. *Classroom Assessment for Student Learning: Doing It Right–Using It Well*. Portland, OR: Pearson.

Cobb, P., and J. Bowers. 1999. "Cognitive and Situated Learning Perspectives in Theory and Practice." *Educational Researcher* 28 (2): 4–15.

Cognition and Technology Group at Vanderbilt. 1997. *The Jasper Project: Lessons in Curriculum, Instruction, Assessment, and Professional Development*. Mahwah, NJ: Lawrence Erlbaum Associates.

Common Core State Standards Initiative. www.corestandards.org/.

Day, J., and K. Wong. 2009. "A Comparative Study of Problem-Based and Lecture-Based Learning in Junior Secondary School Science." *Research in Science Education* 39 (5): 625–42.

De La Paz, S. 2005. "Effects of Historical Reasoning Instruction and Writing Strategy Mastery in Culturally and Academically Diverse Middle School Classrooms." *Journal of Educational Psychology* 97 (2): 139–56.

Dillon, D. R. 1989. "Showing Them That I Want Them to Learn and That I Care About Who They Are: A Microethnography of Social Organization of a Secondary Low-Track English-Reading Classroom." *American Educational Research Journal* 26 (2): 227–59.

Dillon, D. R., D. G. O'Brien, and M. Volkman. 2001. "Reading and Writing to Get Work Done in One Secondary Biology Classroom." In *Constructions of Literacy: Studies of Teaching and Learning in Secondary Classrooms*, edited by E. B. Moje and D. G. O. Brien, 51–75. Mahwah, NJ: Lawrence Erlbaum Associates.

Dobbertin, C. 2013. *Common Core, Unit by Unit: 5 Critical Moves for Implementing Reading Standards Across the Curriculum*. Portsmouth, NH: Heinemann.

Douglas, E., R. Bain, and E. B. Moje. 2009. "Cultural Models of Discipline and Subject Matter: An Examination of Secondary Preservice Teacher Discourse on Content Knowledge." Paper presented at the American Educational Research Association Annual Meeting, April 13. San Diego, CA.

Eccles, J. S., T. F. Adler, R. Futterman, S. B. Goff, C. M. Kaczala, J. L. Meece, and C. Midgley. 1983. "Expectancies, Values, and Academic Behaviors." In *Achievement and Achievement Motivation*, edited by J. T. Spence, 75–146. San Francisco: W. H. Freedman.

Education Week. 2012. "Diplomas Count 2012: High School Redesign." June 7.

eLearning Infographics. May 31, 2016. www.elearninginfographics.com

Ericsson, K. A., R. T. Krampe, and C. Tesch-Römer. 1993. "The Role of Deliberate Practice in the Acquisition of Expert Performance." *Psychological Review* 100 (3): 363–406.

Finkle, S. L., L. L. Torp. 1995. *Introductory Documents.* Available from the Center for Problem-Based Learning, Illinois Math and Science Academy, 1500 West Sullivan Road, Aurora, IL 60506-1000.

Fortus, D., R. C. Dershimer, J. Krajcik, R. W. Marx, and R. Mamlok-Naaman. 2004. "Design-Based Science and Student Learning." *Journal of Research in Science Teaching* 41 (10): 1081–110. doi:10.1002/tea.20040.

Fortus, D., J. Krajcik, R. C. Dershimer, R. W. Marx, and R. Mamlok-Naaman. 2005. "Design-Based Science and Real-World Problem-Solving." *International Journal of Science Education* 27 (7): 855–79. doi:10.1080/09500690500038165.

Fredricks, J. A., P. C. Blumenfeld, and A. H. Paris. 2004. "School Engagement: Potential of the Concept, State of the Evidence." *Review of Educational Research* 74 (1): 59–109.

Freeman, S., S. L. Eddy, M. McDonough, M. K. Smith, N. Okoroafor, H. Jordt, and M. P. Wenderoth. 2014. "Active Learning Increases Student Performance in Science, Engineering, and Mathematics." *Proceedings of the National Academy of Sciences* 111 (23): 8410–415. doi:10.1073/pnas.1319030111.

Freire, P. 1970. *Pedagogy of the Oppressed.* New York: Continuum.

Geier, R., P. C. Blumenfeld, R. W. Marx, J. S. Krajcik, B. Fishman, E. Soloway, and J. Clay-Chambers. 2008. "Standardized Test Outcomes for Students Engaged in Inquiry-Based Science Curricula in the Context of Urban Reform." *Journal of Research in Science Teaching* 45 (8): 922–39. doi:10.1002/tea.20248.

Goodlad, J. I. 1984. *A Place Called School: Prospects for the Future.* New York: McGraw-Hill.

Green, J. L. 1983. "Exploring Classroom Discourse: Linguistic Perspectives on Teaching-Learning Processes." *Educational Psychologist* 18 (3): 180–99.

Greenleaf, C., T. Hanson, J. Herman, C. Litman, S. Madden, R. Rosen, et al. 2009. *Integrating Literacy and Science Instruction in High School Biology: Impact on Teacher Practice, Student Engagement, and Student Achievement.* Grant #0440379. Arlington, VA: National Science Foundation.

Greenleaf, C., R. Schoenbach, C. Cziko, and F. L. Mueller. 2001. "Apprenticing Adolescent Readers to Academic Literacy." *Harvard Educational Review* 71 (1): 79–129.

Guthrie, J. T., and M. H. Davis. 2003. "Motivating Struggling Readers in Middle School Through an Engagement Model of Classroom Practice." *Reading & Writing Quarterly* 19: 59–85.

Guthrie, J. T., L. W. Hoa, A. Wigfield, A. M. Tonks, and K. C. Perencevich. 2006. "From Spark to Fire: Can Situational Reading Interest Lead to Long-Term Reading Motivation?" *Reading Research and Instruction* 45 (2): 91–117.

Guthrie, J., A. Mason-Singh, and C. Coddington. 2012. "Instructional Effects of Concept-Oriented Reading Instruction on Motivation for Reading Information Text in Middle School." In *Adolescents' Engagement in Academic Literacy*, edited by J. Guthrie, A. Wigfield, and S. Lutz Klauda, 155–215. www.corilearning.com/research-publications/2012_adolescents_engagement_ebook.pdf.

Guthrie, J. T., P. Van Meter, A. McCann, A. Wigfield, L. Bennett, C. Poundstone, M.E. Rice, F. Faibisch, B. Hunt, and A. Mitchell. 1996. "Growth in Literacy Engagement: Changes in Motivations and Strategies during Concept-Oriented Reading Instruction." *Reading Research Quarterly* 31 (3): 306–32.

Guthrie, J. T., A. Wigfield, and K. C. Perencevich. 2004. *Motivating Reading Comprehension: Concept-Oriented Reading Instruction*. Mahwah, NJ: Lawrence Erlbaum Associates.

Harmon, L. L., and J. Pegg. 2012. "Literacy Strategies Build Connections Between Introductory Biology Laboratories and Lecture Concepts." *Journal of College Science Teaching* 41 (3): 92–98.

Holt-Reynolds, D. 1992. "Personal History-Based Beliefs as Relevant Prior Knowledge in Course Work." *American Educational Research Journal* 29 (2): 325–49.

James-Burdumy, S., W. Mansfield, J. Deke, N. Carey, J. Lugo-Gil, A. Hershey, A. Douglas, R. Gersten, R. Newman-Gonchar, J. Dimino, B. Faddis, and A. Pendleton. 2009. *Effectiveness of Selected Supplemental Reading Comprehension Interventions: Impacts on a First Cohort of Fifth-Grade Students* (NCEE 2009-4032). Washington, DC: National Center for Education Evaluation and Regional Assistance, Institute of Education Sciences, U.S. Department of Education.

Kemple, J. J., W. Corrin, E. Nelson, T. Salinger, S. Herrmann, and K. Drummond. 2008. *The Enhanced Reading Opportunities Study: Early Impact and Implementation Findings*. The Enhanced Reading Opportunities Study: Early Impact and Implementation Findings (NCEE report no. 2008-4015). Washington, DC: National Center for Education Evaluation and Regional Assistance, Institute of Education Sciences, U.S. Department of Education.

Krajcik, J., P. C. Blumenfeld, R. W. Marx, K. M. Bass, J. Fredricks, and E. Soloway. 1998. "Inquiry in Project-Based Science Classrooms: Initial Attempts by Middle School Students." *The Journal of the Learning Sciences* 7 (3 & 4): 313–50.

Lee, C. D., and A. Spratley. 2010. *Reading in the Disciplines: The Challenges of Adolescent Literacy*. New York: Carnegie Corporation of New York.

Lynch, S. J. 2000. *Equity and Science Education Reform*. Mahwah, NJ: Lawrence Erlbaum Associates.

Medina, J. 2008. *Brain Rules*. Seattle: Pear Press.

Moje, E. B. 2006. "Motivating Texts, Motivating Contexts, Motivating Adolescents: An Examination of the Role of Motivation in Adolescent Literacy Practices and Development." *Perspectives* 32 (3): 10–14.

———. 2007. "Developing Socially Just Subject-Matter Instruction: A Review of the Literature on Disciplinary Literacy." In *Review of Research in Education*, edited by L. Parker, 1–44. Washington, DC: American Educational Research Association.

———. 2008. "Foregrounding the Disciplines in Secondary Literacy Teaching and Learning: A Call for Change." *Journal of Adolescent and Adult Literacy* 52 (2): 96–107.

———. 2010. "Comprehending in the Content Areas: The Challenges of Comprehension, Grades 7–12, and What to Do About Them." In *A Comprehensive Look at Reading Comprehension, K–12*, edited by K. Ganske and D. Fisher, 46-72. New York: Guilford.

———. 2015. "Doing and Teaching Disciplinary Literacy with Adolescent Learners: A Social and Cultural Enterprise." *Harvard Educational Review* 85 (2): 254–78.

Moje, E. B., W. G. Brozo, and J. Haas. 1994. "Portfolios in a High School Classroom: Challenges to Change." *Reading Research and Instruction* 33: 275–92.

Moje, E. B., T. Collazo, R. Carrillo, and R. W. Marx. 2001. "'Maestro, What Is 'Quality?': Language, Literacy, and Discourse in Project-Based Science." *Journal of Research in Science Teaching* 38 (4): 469–96.

Moje, E. B., and C. Lewis. 2007. "Examining Opportunities to Learn Literacy: The Role of Critical Sociocultural Literacy Research." In *Reframing Sociocultural Research on Literacy: Identity, Agency, and Power*, edited by C. Lewis, P. Enciso, and E. B. Moje, 15–48. Mahwah, NJ: Lawrence Erlbaum Associates.

Moje, E. B., D. Peek-Brown, L. M. Sutherland, R. W. Marx, P. Blumenfeld, and J. Krajcik. 2004. "Explaining Explanations: Developing Scientific Literacy in Middle-School Project-Based Science Reforms." In *Bridging the Gap: Improving Literacy Learning for Preadolescent and Adolescent Learners in Grades 4–12*, edited by D. Strickland and D. E. Alvermann, 227–51. New York: Teachers College Press.

Moje, E. B., and J. Speyer. 2008. "The Reality of Challenging Texts in High School Science and Social Studies: How Teachers Can Mediate Comprehension." In *Best Practices in Adolescent Literacy Instruction*, edited by K. Hinchman and H. Sheridan-Thomas, 185–211. New York: Guilford Press.

———. 2014. "Reading Challenging Texts in High School: How Teachers Can Scaffold and Build Close Reading for Real Purposes in the Subject Areas." In *Best Practices in Adolescent Literacy Instruction*, 2nd ed., edited by K. Hinchman and H. Thomas, 207–31. New York: Guilford.

Moje, E. B., D. Stockdill, K. Kim, and H.-J. Kim. 2011. "The Role of Text in Disciplinary Learning." In *Handbook of Reading Research*, Vol. IV, edited by M. Kamil, P. D. Pearson, P. A. Afflerbach, and E. B. Moje, 453–86. Mahwah, NJ: Erlbaum, Taylor & Francis.

Moje, E. B., D. J. Willes, and K. Fassio. 2001. "Constructing and Negotiating Literacy in the Writer's Workshop: Literacy Teaching and Learning in the Seventh Grade." In *Constructions of Literacy: Studies of Teaching and Learning Literacy In and Out of Secondary Classrooms*, edited by E. B. Moje and D. G. O'Brien, 193–212. Mahwah, NJ: Lawrence Erlbaum Associates.

Monte-Sano, C., S. De La Paz, and M. Felton. 2014. *Reading, Thinking, and Writing About History: Teaching Argument Writing to Diverse Learners in the Common Core Classroom, Grades 6–12*. New York: Teachers College Press.

Morris, S. K. 2010. *A Comparison of Learning Outcomes in a Traditional Lecture-Based Versus Blended Course Module Using a Business Simulation with High Cognitive Load*. (PhD), University of San Francisco. http://search.proquest.com. proxy.lib.umich.edu/docview/964172344?accountid=14667 ERIC database.

NCSS. National Curriculum Standards for Social Studies: A Framework for Teaching, Learning, and Assessment. www.socialstudies.org/standards.

NGSS Lead States. 2013. *Next Generation Science Standards: For States, by States*. Washington, DC: National Academies Press. www.nextgenscience.org/.

Norris, S. P., and L. M. Phillips. 2003a. "How Literacy in Its Fundamental Sense Is Central to Scientific Literacy." *Science Education* 87 (2): 224–40.

———. 2003b. "The Public Understanding of Science Information: Communicating, Interpreting, and Applying the Science of Learning." *Education Canada* 43 (2): 25–7, 43.

O'Brien, D. G., and R. A. Stewart. 1990. "Preservice Teachers' Perspectives on Why Every Teacher Is Not a Teacher of Reading: A Qualitative Analysis." *Journal of Reading Behavior* 22 (2): 101–29.

O'Brien, D. G., R. A. Stewart, and E. B. Moje. 1995. "Why Content Literacy Is Difficult to Infuse into the Secondary School: Complexities of Curriculum, Pedagogy, and School Culture." *Reading Research Quarterly* 30 (3): 442–63.

O'Brien, T. 2009. *The Things They Carried*. New York: Mariner Books.

Palincsar, A. S., and A. L. Brown. 1984. "Reciprocal Teaching of Comprehension-Fostering and Comprehension-Monitoring Activities." *Cognition & Instruction* 1 (2): 117–75.

Palincsar, A. S., and S. J. Magnusson. 2001. "The Interplay of First-Hand and Text-Based Investigations to Model and Support the Development of Scientific Knowledge and Reasoning." In *Cognition and Instruction: 25 Years of Progress*, edited by S. M. Carver and D. Klahr, 152–93. Mahwah, NJ: Lawrence Erlbaum Associates.

Pearson, P. D., E. B. Moje, and C. Greenleaf. 2010. "Literacy and Science: Each in the Service of the Other." *Science* 328: 459–63.

Piaget, J. 1977. *The Essential Piaget*. New York: Basic Books.

Rogoff, B., and J. Lave. 1984. *Everyday Cognition: Its Development in Social Context*. Cambridge, MA: Harvard University Press.

Rumelhart, D. 1994. "Toward an Interactive Model of Reading." In *Theoretical Models and Processes of Reading*, 4th ed., edited by R. B. Ruddel, M. R. Ruddell, and H. Singer, 864–94. Newark, DE: International Reading Association.

Schoenbach, R., and C. Greenleaf. 2009. "Fostering Adolescents' Engaged Academic Literacy." In *Handbook of Adolescent Literacy Research*, edited by L. Christenbury, R. Bomer, and P. Smagorinsky, 98–112. New York: Guilford Press.

Schoenbach, R., C. Greenleaf, C. Cziko, and L. Hurwitz, L. 1999. *Reading for Understanding: A Guide to Improving Reading in Middle and High School Classrooms*. The Jossey-Bass Education Series. San Francisco: Jossey-Bass Publishers.

Schwerdt, G., and A. C. Wuppermann. 2011. "Sage on the Stage." Education Next 11 (3).

Scott, F. S. 1999. *The Great Gatsby*. New York: Scribner.

Sizer, T. R. 1984. *Horace's Compromise: The Dilemma of the American High School*. Boston: Houghton Mifflin.

———. 2004. *Horace's Compromise: The Dilemma of the American High School*, 4th ed. New York: Houghton Mifflin.

Smagorinsky, P., ed. 2014. *Teaching Dilemmas and Solutions in Content-Area Literacy, Grades 6–12*. Thousand Oaks, CA: Sage.

Sturtevant, E. G., V. P. Duling, and R. E. Parson. 2000. "'I've Run a 4,000-Person Organization—and It's Not Nearly This Intense': A Three-Year Case Study of Content Literacy in High School Mathematics." In *Constructions of Literacy: Studies of Literacy Teaching and Learning in Secondary Classrooms and Schools*, edited by E. B. Moje and D. G. O'Brien. 77–103. Mahwah, NJ: Lawrence Erlbaum Associates.

Tovani, C. 2011. *So What Do They Really Know? Assessment That Informs Teaching and Learning*. Portland, ME: Stenhouse.

Vygotsky, L. S. 1986. *Thought and Language*. Translated by A. Kozulin. Cambridge, MA: Massachusetts Institute of Technology Press.

Wade, S. E., and E. B. Moje. 2000. "The Role of Text in Classroom Learning." In *The Handbook of Research on Reading*, Vol. III, edited by M. Kamil, P. B. Mosenthal, R. Barr, and P. D. Pearson, 609–27. Mahwah, NJ: Lawrence Erlbaum Associates.

Ward, J. D., and C. L. Lee. 2004. "Teaching Strategies for FCS: Student Achievement in Problem-Based Learning Versus Lecture-Based Instruction." *Journal of Family and Consumer Sciences* 96 (1): 73–76.

Wigfield, A., J. S. Eccles, and D. Rodriguez. 1998. "The Development of Children's Motivation in School Contexts." In *Review of Research in Education,* Vol. 23, edited by P. D. Pearson and A. Iran-Nejad, 73–118. Washington, DC: American Educational Research Association.

Wiggins, G. 2014a. "A PS to the Guest Post on Shadowing HS Students (and the Author Revealed)." October 19. https://grantwiggins.wordpress.com/2014/10/19/a-ps-to-the-guest-post-on-shadowing-hs-students-and-the-author-revealed/.

———. 2014b. "A Veteran Teacher Turned Coach Shadows 2 Students for 2 Days—A Sobering Lesson Learned." October 10. https://grantwiggins.wordpress.com/2014/10/10/a-veteran-teacher-turned-coach-shadows-2-students-for-2-days-a-sobering-lesson-learned/.

Wineburg, S. S. 1998. "Reading Abraham Lincoln: An Expert/Expert Study in the Interpretation of Historical Texts." *Cognitive Science* 22 (3): 319–46.